England and Ireland Since 1800

PATRICK O'FARRELL

England and Ireland Since 1800

OXFORD UNIVERSITY PRESS
LONDON OXFORD NEW YORK
1975

Oxford University Press

LONDON OXFORD NEW YORK

GLASGOW TORONTO MELBOURNE WELLINGTON

CAPE TOWN IBADAN NAIROBI DAR ES SALAAM LUSAKA ADDIS ABABA

DELHI BOMBAY CALCUTTA MADRAS KARACHI LAHORE DACCA

KUALA LUMPUR SINGAPORE HONG KONG TOKYO

Paperback ISBN 0 19 289045 X

Casebound ISBN 0 19 215814 7

© Oxford University Press 1975

REPL

Set by Malvern Typesetting Services Ltd
and printed in Great Britain by
Richard Clay & Co Ltd, Bungay, Suffolk

Contents

Preface

I T is impossible to write about this subject without arousing emotion. Perhaps it is also impossible to write about it without being misunderstood. If either of these things should occur in regard to this book it would hardly be surprising, for much of it is concerned with emotions and misunderstandings as active forces within history and human affairs. And of course what one person may regard as prejudice, another may see as legitimate opinion.

However, experience suggests that a brief personal statement is necessary. I am by birth and upbringing a New Zealander, and still regard myself as one, with whatever qualifications have been induced by nearly twenty years living in Australia. Against the happy experience of a predominantly English colonial environment in New Zealand from the 1930s to the 1950s, I can set, no less happily, the less Anglicized atmosphere of Australia from then until now. To this must be added an earlier immediate family world with something of an Irish flavour, and two years spent living in Ireland, 1965-6 and 1972-3.

I am at one with, and grateful for, all these elements in my experience, and in rebellion neither for nor against any of them. Not that I claim detachment: I am deeply concerned by recent events in Ireland, but this concern derives from involvement in mankind and from Christian principle, and not from any partisan position other than those. Because I argue that violence and prejudice have been effective forces in Anglo-Irish affairs it should not be presumed that I have some brief for them or for any other of the actions or opinions I describe. I detest violence, as well as ignorance, prejudice, irresponsibility and other similar aspects of human behaviour, but it is not the business of the historian to engage in continual explicit denunciations of humanity's sins and shortcomings. He must assume that his reader shares with him such basic human values and sympathies as will allow learning from the past rather than some futile reproaching of it.

I have deliberately avoided drawing on my previous book on Anglo-Irish relations, *Ireland's English Question. Anglo-Irish Relations 1534–1970* (Batsford, 1971). This is not because I have abandoned the arguments presented there. The present study is another and much shorter book, and it seemed more useful to devote it to other ways of reviewing the relationship, rather than to recapitulate in summary ideas already in print.

The usual Irish concept of the power that ruled them, and with which they were in conflict, was that of 'England' and the 'English', rather than that of 'Britain' and the 'British': it was an image into which the Scots and the Welsh intruded very little. Being the wider term, 'Britain' was acceptable to Unionists but not to nationalists, at least prior to their having their own state. Given this book's concern with the imagery of difference and contrast, 'England' has been used throughout, unless obvious geography or the context of usage render that inappropriate.

Many aspects of the themes surveyed here seem to me worthy of much more extensive, detailed, and profound study than I have been able to give them. That such a survey is possible at all, is due to the relatively recent development in Ireland, England, and America of first-rate historical investigation of important elements in Anglo-Irish relations: my indebtedness to this scholarship is substantial. Mr A. L. Schuller of Oxford University Press first discerned that it might be possible and worthwhile to write a book with this particular angle and emphasis. The University of New South Wales provided conditions and opportunities which made it possible for me to write: in Ireland, I am similarly indebted to University College, Dublin, and also Trinity College, Dublin. The Library staff of the University of New South Wales provided practical assistance of great value. At the intellectual level of stimulus and criticism, and the suggestion of ideas and sources, I have received more help than I can detail. To make a general acknowledgement, I wish to thank my colleagues and students here, and those in Dublin, at both University College and Trinity. I am responsible for the inadequacies of this book, but they would have been greater had it not been for the care and criticism it received from my wife.

August 1974   Patrick O'Farrell
                              School of History,
                              University of New South Wales

1
Matters of History

IT has often been remarked that there is a sense in which Ireland has no history: as popularly received, all history has remained current affairs. This has been so particularly in matters of Anglo-Irish and Protestant-Catholic relations, where Cromwell, William of Orange, the Penal Laws, the famine, Fenianism, and a host of other persons and events, were all telescoped into one remembered yesterday. In 1865, John Blake Dillon informed a Parliamentary Committee that he considered the land tenure situation in Ireland to have been vitally affected by 'very recent . . . and very extensive confiscations'. When had these taken place? 'In the time of Cromwell,' Dillon replied, adding that 'Any act that has an important bearing upon the present condition of the country is sufficiently recent to justify me in describing it as very recent'.

This being so, it could be argued that the basic character of Anglo-Irish relations, and of relations between Protestants and Catholics within Ireland, was determined long before 1800. This argument might refer to the cultural friction which developed from the time of initial encounters, or to specific historical developments dividing the experience of the two peoples—such as the Reformation—or even to topography: a landscape of mountains and bogs made it impossible for the English to conquer the whole country, and all subsequent difficulties stem from this incomplete subjugation. To accept such propositions as tenable is not, however, to consign subsequent history to the role of protracted epilogue. The questions remain, why did such earlier factors become continuing determinants, and could their influence have been minimized or even avoided later in that period of closest relationship between England and Ireland, from 1800?

Although the general history of Anglo-Irish relations before 1800 is not under review here, some of its aspects are of particular relevance to the themes of this book.

Up to the Reformation, English activity in Ireland was desultory and restricted. English claims in, and over Ireland might be said to have begun with the invasion by Henry II in 1171, but the pursuit of conquest was limited and erratic. Celtic Ireland remained almost untouched, while the English monarchy had neither the power nor inclination to pursue rigorously any policy which might conquer, pacify or govern all of Ireland. However from the beginning of the relationship, its keynote was firmly established as that of English expansionist aggression meeting with consistent resistance within Ireland.

The question of why this aggression took place, and why it was resisted, is answerable partly in terms of the particular and immediate historical circumstances: there was nothing unique or abnormal about such conflicts in the Europe of the time. However, another important aspect of the answer does have enduring significance — that which emphasizes culture clash.

Several recent studies have taken this approach. Professor E. Estyn Evans sees the 'personality' of Ireland (its habitat, heritage, and history) as in conflict with England since the later middle ages: the derogatory image of the Irish in English history dates from Giraldus Cambrensis in 1185. W.R. Jones explains this image as a consequence of the encounter between Anglo-Norman and Angevin England ('richer, more highly centralized, feudal and manorial') and Celtic societies ('tribal, mobile, disaggregative'). The outcome was English hostility and contempt towards Celtic societies seen as inferior, barbarous, and primitive. The portrayal of Celtic society as savage, with attendant poverty, indolence, and brutality, became entrenched in English imagery from medieval times, and provided a moral justification for continued English efforts to dominate or destroy the Celts. Jones sees this as illustration of a continuing theme in world history—the competition of rival cultures, dramatized by the stronger and better organized one into a collision between 'civilization' and 'barbarism'. Cultural differences were 'sharpened, exaggerated, and moralized by English critics': to the English, such Irish differences exhibited moral inferiority.

Dr Nicholas Canny has investigated this theme in relation to Tudor colonization in Ireland. Coming with pre-conceived ideas of a barbaric society, English adventurers tailored the Irish to fit these ideas, despite contradictory evidence. Thus, in order to justify their conduct, they set about convincing themselves—and England—that the Irish were pagans, and thus uncivilized. The practice of transhumance was inflated into proof that the Irish were nomads, and hence barbarians. So it was justifiable for a superior people to subdue them, with the declared purpose of civilizing them: if they resisted (as they did) this proved their intransigent barbarism and justified their extermination.

Dr Canny links this image of the Irish with the English self-image: the adventurers and colonists were unsure of themselves, anxious to retain a view of their own behaviour as that of civilized Christians. Moral justification for their claim to superiority (and to conquest of Irish land) was sustained by imputing inferiority to the native inhabitants. They deliberately did not seek to understand the Irish, and remained obstinately blind to such characteristics as contradicted their convenient image, for that image was necessary for their own self-regard, and for the respectable continuance of their dominance. One particular long-term legacy of this self-deception was the idea, which became ingrained in English thinking, that all Ireland's barbarisms stemmed from Ireland's ruling class and leaders (which the English displaced) while the peasantry was by nature good-hearted and docile. So the Englishman could depict himself as a benefactor, bringing to the mass of hitherto oppressed people true liberty and civilization under English government. And such resistance as the Englishman met in

Ireland could be attributed not to any real popular antagonism, but to the perverse influence of a few old or would-be Irish leaders.

Ned Lebow, surveying the writing on Irish history by English historians of the twelfth to the nineteenth centuries also sees adverse English judgements as illustrating the compulsion felt by colonizers to depict the colonized people as primitive and inferior, with morality and civilization the monopoly of the colonizers. He demonstrates how such judgements were taken unquestioningly by each generation of historians from that previous to it, thus establishing a tradition which appeared both venerable and authoritative.

Generally, the English habit of regarding the Irish as inferior was of the greatest importance in determining the relationship at all stages of its existence. As well as inducing and sanctioning continued English dominance, it embedded Irish resistance. It militated against any mutual acceptance of differences, and fostered the confrontation of crude hostile stereotypes. It was the English insistence that Ireland was a barbarous country which drove the Irish to construct, so as to sustain their own pride, a romantic and consoling counter-image, in which ancient Ireland was displayed as a land of saints and scholars, warlike but chivalrous Celtic heroes, and monks of great learning and Christian zeal, the whole island a light in a dark world. This construct, developed throughout the nineteenth century, often with considerable scholarship, gave Ireland a sense of proud history, of achievement now denied. So was nurtured both a sense of grievance—at present deprivation—and a highly imaginative, heroic view of the past, a dream world which was a constant stimulus to romantic idealism in the present. The harsh unflattering English view of traditional Irish society eventually provoked an Irish interpretation: if the English interpretation was a suitable ideology for domination, the Irish was one suitable for rebellion.

Of course, ancient Irish history was only one area of difference: later history provided ample material to support opposing views of the same facts. From about 1534, the circumstances of the Reformation and the growth of monarchic power in England led the Tudors to attempt the complete conquest of Ireland. This was motivated by an enduring theme in England's Irish policies, the wish to ensure, in a hostile world, that the adjacent island did not become a base for England's enemies. By 1603 this conquest was complete, in that English government had been substituted for the authority systems of Gaelic Ireland, but it was a failure in the realm of popular acceptance. Most of the inhabitants of Ireland refused to accept the reformed religion of the English state and maintained a firm adherence to Catholicism, a development of profound political significance as well as religious, for it entailed the refusal to accept the legitimacy of the English Protestant monarchy. Thereafter, in English eyes, the Irish were identified with disloyalty and subversion, wedded to a religion of ignorance, tyranny, and superstition, governable only by coercion.

This identification of the Irish as a menace to English power was reinforced by the experience of the seventeenth-century—Irish rebellion in 1641, followed by disturbances and warfare put down vigorously by Oliver Cromwell in 1649, but not ended until the victory of William of Orange at Aughrim in 1691. The fifty-year conflict between Catholic Ireland and Protestant England from 1641 to 1691 established an apparently inexhaustible reservoir of hatred drawn on by both sides. Cromwell became, for the Irish, a symbol and epitome of an English policy of extermination and confiscation. Colonists from Britain—the Scots Presbyterians who came to Ulster from 1607, the English and Scots who came after the Cromwellian land settlement of 1652—bequeathed their experiences and fears at that time as a harsh triumphalist intransigence firm against any concessions to the Catholics and Celts among whom they had come to live.

The outcome was the Protestant Ireland of the eighteenth century, ruled by an ascendancy which, by religious tests, excluded Catholics from any position of power or influence. Although this ascendancy, as a small minority, relied ultimately on the backing of the London government, it sought, in the 1780s, to exercise a degree of self-government. Its inability to govern Ireland was demonstrated by the outbreak of rebellion in 1798. This led to the Act of Union of 1800, which merged Ireland with Great Britain into the United Kingdom, and gave Ireland representation in the Westminster parliament, a relationship which lasted until its partial dissolution in 1921 when the twenty-six southern counties of Ireland became the Irish Free State, the six northern ones remaining with the United Kingdom.

The early period of Union saw the rapid emergence of serious disagreement and conflict. There was the matter of the continuance of the Union itself: the repeal agitation of the 1840s represented constitutional pressure towards ending it, the rebellions of 1848 and 1867 were violent attempts to destroy the linkage. These Irish efforts to dissolve the Union met adamant English determination to maintain it. Then there was the matter of basic survival. The great famine of 1845-9 put into question in Ireland the validity of a government which failed to cope with that disaster, and the accompanying and subsequent mass migration appeared to the Irish to reveal English administration as utterly malign. As well, there was the question of freedom for the Catholic religion, an aim pursued successfully in regard to Catholic emancipation in 1829, and disestablishment of the Anglican Church in Ireland in 1869, but without success in regard to Catholic education, a claim to which the British government remained resistant, at the university level, until 1908. And there was the matter of land, believed by the native Irish tenants to be theirs, but formally owned by landlords who were in the main English or Anglo-Irish or Ulster Protestant. On this issue, the British parliament remained unyielding until limited concessions were made to tenants in 1870.

From 1870, these themes of Irish discontent with English rule came to group around a growing powerful movement for Home Rule, backed by a popular peasant agitation. This movement gained much ground, securing both reforming legislation in regard to specific grievances and apparent gradual progress towards its ultimate Home Rule objective. However, in doing so, it brought to the surface (though this was insufficiently realized at the time) a profound and most serious division existing within Ireland itself. Nationalist and Catholic Ireland desired some form of home rule. Protestant Ireland, of Scots and Anglo-Irish descent, most powerful in north-east Ulster, wanted continuance of the union with Britain. The emergence of this division, its elements seeking irreconcilable ends, presented an irresolvable problem to British politicians, themselves divided on the issue. But some adjustment of the relationship was made imperative by the re-emergence, in circumstances of wartime crisis, of the revolutionary demand for severance of the Anglo-Irish connection expressed in the Easter 1916 rebellion, and in the swift subsequent decline into what amounted to Anglo-Irish war. The British responded with the device of partition.

At that time, in 1920-1, this was regarded by all parties to it, as unsatisfactory (though for different reasons), but the new relationship substantially endured until it was called in question by the events in Northern Ireland since 1968. It had, however, been already considerably modified by the gradual rejection by the southern Irish state of its initial dominion status, a development which reached terminal formality with its unilateral declaration in 1949 that it was a republic: this did not alter the practical relationship with Great Britain, which remained on a favoured commonwealth level. The crisis which began in Northern Ireland in 1968 was originally a domestic one, stemming from internal discriminatory policies pursued by Protestant administrations, central and local, against Catholic citizens. Once begun, conflict soon reverted to deriving its impetus from historic fears and grievances, so as to resurrect in a contemporary setting the bitterly antagonistic elements whose existence had led to the initial partition. The Northern Ireland government's inability to maintain law and order soon involved British policy, because of Britain's ultimate sovereignty over Northern Ireland, and then British armed force, and so, in consequence, the whole question of Britain's relationship with Ireland, north and south, was revived.

Particularly in the matter of emotions, and in the sense that it was leftover business from a problem avoided rather than solved in 1920-1, there was much that was old in the revived Northern Ireland problem. There was also much that was new. The two states that shared Ireland had been in existence for half a century and had developed their own sense of identity within that time and geographical confines. And Britain, far from wishing to dominate and determine the Irish scene, wished that the Irish would (or could) conduct their own affairs properly and peacefully. This last was an old wish in a new context. That it should come painfully alive again, in the most distressing circumstances, seemed to many in Britain inexplicable, absurd, and unfair.

In the minds of men, as well as in the realm of politics, the nature of the relationship between England and Ireland has long been the subject of conflict, controversy, and a wide variety of explanations. The attempt to understand it has led some to utter certainty that they have discovered the key—colonialism, religion, economics or whatever—while others have succumbed to a confusion and uncertainty no less complete. No other of England's historical relationships has generated such protracted and intense difficulties, nor produced so much emotion, exasperation, and bewilderment— nor so many differing plans for some solution.

Perhaps the reasons for this are obvious—the long history and present continuance of unsettled relations, geographical proximity, deep cultural differences between peoples living in close contact, the mutually corruptive effects of an imperial situation, and so on. Add to this the consequences flowing from the existence of a poor and rural island within the orbit of the greatest imperial, industrial, and urban power: here were problems of poverty and politics, problems in the better adjustment of human affairs, problems of the clash of values, interests, and ideas, all of which had wide human application and deep controversial potential. In these circumstances, it is natural that the relationship between England and Ireland has been subject to a wide variety of interpretations.

Such analyses could be reviewed simply as a reflection of a multi-faceted historical predicament, but their function has also been dynamic. To a vital extent, Anglo-Irish affairs have been not only conducted within the realm of imagery but determined by images. Conflicting perceptions of reality, conflicting ideas about what ought to be reality, illusions and distortions, hopes and visions, constitute much of the substance of the relationship, interacting with the more tangible realities of events and economics. The approach of this book derives from the conclusion that in this particular case, pursuit of the historical truth is best served by the assumption that there were two valid 'realities'—one English, the other Irish. Appreciation of this duality—and not the assumption that one element has a monopoly of historical truth—is necessary to understand the relationship. It may be that Ireland's attitude towards the English connection had justice and right on its side, but the consequent implication that England's maintainance of the connection derived simply from injustice and unrighteousness is not historically acceptable or even respectable.

A major concern of this book is to display the images which were believed to be the reality: if the emphasis is more on English images of the Irish, this is because it was those which were the more powerful in determining events and attitudes.

Twice in this century—between 1910 and 1921, and from 1968—events in Ireland have degenerated into crisis, apparently insoluble short of protracted violence. Explanations of this have tended to have a common core in their stress on the legacy of history. Marxists, nationalists, Unionists, liberals, religionists, secularists all point to history as a vital factor in explaining what has happened, creating an overall impression that the present is in the iron grip of the past: history is tendered as almost sufficient explanation for history. However important history was in determining what happened between Ireland and England, the question will remain — why was history so important? It is given particular point because the relationship was so thickly populated with vivid men, and marked by dramatic events they apparently contrived: are these large personalities merely acting out parts determined by the historical script? And what of violence? Did the historical script direct that there should be, from time to time, collapse into bloody *impasse*? Was there only one possible historical scenario?

Those men, English and Irish, who were concerned with the relationship between the two peoples, were not operating within the confines of some classic unreformed tyranny from which escape could be by violence only. As the nineteenth century wore on, they debated within a developing system of responsible and increasingly democratic government, based on a widening electorate, and on procedures of public discussion and popular will. Resort to violence was testimony that this pacific system had failed to resolve the problems that sprang from the relationship. This reflects not only the inadequacy of the men involved in the system, but particularly the inadequacy of the images they had of each other and of the problems they faced.

Crises of any magnitude are usually the culminating points of periods of degenerative historical development. The actual point of crisis may be determined by immediate factors, even trivial or chance ones, but the environment of crisis, the atmosphere which awaits that flash-point, is the outcome of the gradual exhaustion of historical alternatives. The concept of viable alternatives is vital to the democratic process, most fundamentally at the level of alternative governments. However, the possibility of alternative policies and decisions, the availability of choice between one course and another, or merely between fast and slow pace, is present at every level of governmental activity—or rather, it is present until an actual choice is made, or the opportunity to make it passes, until one alternative is pursued, others rejected or neglected. The exercising of choice produces, of course, a new situation which may offer a further set of alternatives, but certain sequences of choice (or of failures to choose) establish a pattern whereby future choice is progressively constricted, eventually to the degree of elimination. The outcome is the gradual restriction of the possibilities of a historical situation, so that ultimately a single outcome becomes inescapable.

While such an imprisonment of events bears, superficially, an inevitablist complexion, it is, in fact, quite the opposite. Far from being the product of necessary historical laws or processes, it is the legacy of a succession of operative human wills, the end point of deliberate decisions or of failures to decide; that is, the consequence of individual attitudes and actions moving in usual human ways. The relationship between England and Ireland bears ample evidence of being the victim of such processes of exhaustion of historical alternatives, leading to confrontation irresolvable short of the test of force. Seen thus, the history of Anglo-Irish relations is not the history of inevitable conflict. It becomes a story of how images, which produce misunderstanding, hostile emotions and mistakes, can weaken and destroy, firstly powers of judgement, and then all areas of choice short of violence. It is an illusion endemic to the processes of democracy that for every problem there is an appropriate pacific solution: problems may pass beyond the point of such solution if the chance to implement it is not seen and taken.

Widespread and active consciousness of the previous history of the relationship between England and Ireland was very much a nineteenth-century development. That awakening, however, was located much more in Ireland than in England: while Ireland, both nationalist and Unionist became conscious of its past, England remained largely ignorant of it. Within Ireland, the relationship with England came to be both assailed and defended on grounds not so much of principle or present operation as on past performance. The use of the past as a point of reference for the future tied forward thinking in Ireland to an unhappy history in which conflict, fear, and grievance had been prominent. Irish radicalism, both nationalist and Unionist, was sustained by its images of precise and particular historical events and people. It looked back, not forward, and its cult of history had at least two important effects. It actively fostered whatever tendency history has to repeat itself, and its apparently conservative orientation, obsessed with the past, produced a constant tendency in England to underestimate gravely the strength and tenacity of its radical potential.

The concentration by historians on Ireland's challenge and England's response has tended to impose an Irish frame of judgement on a relationship which needs an English dimension for its better understanding. There are however other, no less compelling reasons, for attending to that dimension. That element in the population of mainland Britain which was of Irish birth or descent exerted a major influence as image-maker in determining the general character of Anglo-Irish relations. The English and the Scots formed much of their estimate of the Irish from those they encountered in Britain, particularly Irish workers, but also politicians, priests, intellectuals, and entertainers. The Irish in Britain remained a continuing stimulus to impressions and attitudes vital to an understanding of the British reaction to agitation from across the Irish Sea. The present outlook of militant Ulster Protestants, now seen in Britain as so reprehensible and troublesome, displays in an extreme form attitudes prevalent — indeed orthodox — within Britain itself at least up to the First World War: the current Northern Ireland situation represents in extreme and in microcosm, a residuum of what the atmosphere of Anglo-Irish relations once was.

An English angle on the relationship is important also in regard to the question of where and why crucial breakdowns in the relationship took place. A central illustration is the sharply contrasting attitudes to the Act of Union of 1800.

Irish obsession, passion, and agitation over matters relating to the Union often encountered English incomprehension, lethargy, and indifference. This was a natural, if most irritating reflection of the power realities of the relationship. In the last resort of power, England determined the relationship and if apparrent neglect enraged Ireland, Irish demands that England pay attention incensed Englishmen who saw them as absurd. More specifically, there is much to support the view that the key to an explanation of the ultimate collapse into major violence lies within the politics of England, particularly within the history of the Tory party, and in the failure of the Liberal government to respond adequately to the Ulster challenge to Home Rule—politicing immediately productive of the 1910-21 crisis, and eventually of that since 1968. The accusation of Tory infamy and Liberal decomposition, given scholarly form as long ago as George Dangerfield's *The Strange Death of Liberal England* (1935), has tended to be weighed too lightly, probably because the history of Anglo-Irish relations has been cast in the pattern of challenge and response, to the neglect of the processes of degeneration and collapse: the Irish view has perhaps exaggerated the power of the nationalist challenge in effecting change; English political thinking has questioned the validity of that challenge rather than the appropriateness of the response, or the situation in which it was made.

Concern with the English scene is also justified by the strong tendency—natural given the intimate but subordinate nature of the connection—for Irish affairs to become the victim of English politics and English political machinery. At the simplest level this meant that Irish legislation was often decided by men ignorant of Ireland and motivated by irrelevant if not conflicting English interests and attitudes. More specifically it could be argued, for instance, that, from 1885 the fortunes of Home Rule were dependent on the fate and political interests of the Liberal party—or of the Tory party. But the processes of victimization were more extensive and subtle than this.

British politics showed a constant proclivity to translate practical Irish problems into English principles. Thus, the question of Irish land reform raised the spectre of expropriation and communism, famine relief seemed to challenge the basic tenets of accepted economic orthodoxy, Parnell's tactics in forcing parliamentary attention towards Irish issues were received as a fundamental threat to the constitutional machinery, Home Rule called into question the powers of the House of Lords and the future of the Empire. Ireland's problems were, in the main, different from and external to those of England. Any legislative solution lay in externalizing and particularizing them. Instead, they were consistently internalized and generalized. Nor should the matter of direct and deliberate English interference be minimized in seeking the causes of vital developments in the relationship. C. C. O'Brien has instanced a crucial case: if the revolutionary crisis of 1916–21 can be traced back in origin to the consequences of the fall of Parnell, the decisive factor in that fall was Gladstone's ultimatum, an English not an Irish contrivance. Professor D.A. Hamer has drawn attention to that group of interpretations which see the Irish question as a safety valve or testing ground for English ideas, internal tensions, and political stratagems: he investigated the possibility that Irish questions were employed by Liberal politicians for narrowly party purposes—those of achieving party unity, and of evading the need to confront issues of English reform.

It became Irish nationalist orthodoxy to blame England for all the ills of Ireland. Not only unpopular policies, but unfavourable economic facts, the very paucity of natural resources, were taken as evidence of deliberate English exploitation. Social and economic changes, led and exemplified by England, but not peculiar to her, indeed the whole process of modernization and change, industrialization and urbanization, came to be received in Ireland as malignantly anti-Irish. Irish conservatism opposed progress and change as being English. England became the image of all that Ireland should not be. It was the City of Mammon from which the Godly Irish must preserve their land and their hearts. The image of an ideal Ireland held, for instance, by Eamon de Valera —prosperous, but mainly rural, concerned with the family, with right living, and the things of the spirit— developed in reaction against what Irish nationalists took to be the essence of England—the pursuit of wealth, sensation, and sin.

The challenge which Ireland represented to English government provoked tardy and inadequate practical responses, but far back into the history of the connection individual Englishmen can be found who were unhappy about those responses. Their number increased from the Union: thus Sydney Smith in 1807: 'The moment the very name of Ireland is mentioned, the English seem to bid adieu to common feeling, common prudence, and common sense, and to act with the barbarity of tyrants and the fatuity of idiots.' From the 1860s such judgements by individual Englishmen were sufficiently prevalent as to constitute a significant unease about the Irish connection, which increased to widespread dismay towards the end of the Anglo-Irish war in 1920-1. However, this did not betoken any widespread English awakening to full understanding or acceptance of Irish claims. The negotiations and decisions which produced the partition of Ireland, and dominion status for its southern counties in 1920-1, reflected no real grasp, in the decisive areas of British power, either of the passionate reality of Irish nationalism or of the intense depth of Ulster exclusivism. Instead, the impulses were exasperation, the wish to be rid of embarrassment and nuisance, and the exigencies of opportunist power and party politics. It is not surprising that the settlement arranged then eventually revealed its impermanence. The past re-emerged to revenge itself on the present.

That Irish behaviour, and beliefs—such as the simple historical equation that English oppression equalled Ireland's woes—were unintelligible to the English mind is explained by the sharp divergence between English and Irish views of their shared history. The basic difference was in the amount of attention each gave the other: while England loomed very large in Irish history, Ireland seldom obtruded in the story of England. And whereas England dominated recent Irish history as enemy and oppressor, Ireland hardly appeared at all in the English version, or as merely a troublesome footnote: this being how history was popularly received by the English, they were both unaware of Irish hatred and of the historical reasons for it. In England, the popular consciousness of history, and its school content, were, by the later nineteenth century, of a tradition of invincible English superiority, the establishment by England of a code of urbane and progressive civilization, and a sense that the present was a golden age, the apex of human progress with England herself in the lead. The Irish consciousness of history placed England in a very different perspective, and saw Ireland's golden age as having existed over a thousand years before, when Ireland, it was believed, was the centre of European Christian civilization.

English ignorance and incomprehension of the Irish view of history denied them an understanding of Irish nationalism to which that historical view was central. Not only did the Irish nationalists construct an idealized and pure image of ancient glory—which must be restored—but they mounted a determined assault upon the despotism of fact, glorying in their historical humiliation at the hands of the English and celebrating themselves as noble victims in sorrowful songs and sermons. Around the heroic legends and savage substance of the past, its defeats, its deaths, and degradation, Ireland's poets, preachers, politicians, and propagandists wove a romantic image of heroic suffering and unconquerable virtuous endurance, and combined this with the exaltation of a brilliant lost ideal.

History was no less important to those in Ireland who wished to retain the English connection, Protestant Unionists mainly in the Ulster counties. While the majority of the Irish treasured history because it showed that the connection must be broken, Protestant Unionists valued history because it proved that it was imperative that the connection be maintained. The myths and realities of seventeenth-century experience continued to sustain intransigent contemporary attitudes. Crucial to understanding this reliance on, and constant reference to past events is to realize that these events are not regarded as history at all. The idea that history is the story of change is explicitly rejected, and thus, past events have as much weight in forming contemporary judgements as present observation — indeed more, for while today's appearances may be deceptive, yesterday's events have taken clear form. In 1917 Ernest Hamilton in baring *The Soul of Ulster* laid it down that:

'. . . the basic nature of the native Irish Celt remains the same today as it was in the days of Elizabeth . . . The fundamental idea at the back of the Ulsterman's attitude is that what has once happened may well happen again . . . the soul of the native Irish has not at the present day changed by the width of a hair from what it was in 1641, and again in 1798 . . .'

This was why remembrance of old Catholic and Celtic atrocities and rebellions was imperative, not simply as nursing past wrongs but as a warning for the present. It was seen as relevant evidence of present or future intentions. This approach to history was, like the nationalist one, inaccessible to counter-argument. However embellished or mythologized, there was a core of fact in these historical visions, and that core made them dynamic visions for those who experienced them: it was futile for the uninitiated or the unconverted to deride or deplore. History as the basis for contemporary hopes or contemporary fears, and as the bolster of particular social and political attitudes, was in essence simply another factor in current affairs, one peculiarly resistant to any change; what were so often false, distorted, partial, and dead images were taken to be living immutable facts.

2

Images

UNDER the Union, as before, the relationship between England and Ireland was one of subjection, met by continued criticism and recurrent resistance. Immediately one seeks to expand or explain this simplicity, a tortuous maze of images obtrudes, images no less important than reality, dynamic images 'that yet/Fresh images beget'. All facets of the Anglo-Irish relationship were decisively influenced by powerful mental representations—presumptions, conceptions, impressions, understandings—to which reality was subordinated. Substantially it was a relationship conducted on the level of stereotypes and prejudices.

The Union of 1800 imported the relationship with Ireland into the centre of the British political system. Where before Ireland might be regarded as virtually foreign affairs, its political integration gave it direct domestic dimensions for Britain, and the persistent difficulties encountered in dealing with it compelled attention to explaining and understanding what was taking place and why.

The culture clash situation, as has been suggested, disposed the superior power both to exalt its own virtues, and to reject the subject culture as either not worth understanding, or as amply understood in negative and derogatory terms. This evaluation bred bitter resentment, and the impulse, within the subject culture, to both prove its own worth and to argue that what the conquerors saw as their own virtues were in reality vices. This abrasion was exacerbated by the factor of distance: the two cultures were close enough for constant friction, too distant to mingle easily.

Then there were the consequences of the preponderance of British power. A relationship in which superior power always remained an ultimate potential solvent did not elicit understanding as an imperative need: it could well be easier to simply discipline the Irish rather than to attempt to discover what agitated them. The availability to Britain of resort to coercion did much to vitiate and delay the development of understanding. It entrenched the view that the only treatment the Irish understood was coercion and convinced the Irish that the only policy of which Britain was capable was coercion. *The Times* laid it down in 1867: '. . . the Englishman's view of the question is that which must prevail in the end, whatever temporary and partial expedients may be applied.' If that was what the relationship must boil down to, in an English view, then it was on the field of force that the Irish must challenge it, if they were determined to do so.

The power of artificial, partial, and convenient depictions of reality was particularly great in a situation where experience of reality at firsthand was severely restricted by ignorance and unfamiliarity. Relatively few Englishmen knew Ireland other than indirectly, through what they read or were told: those who had visited Ireland tended to know it only in its Anglo-Irish aspect. In 1880, M.F. Cusack reported that he had found in England 'an extraordinary and almost total ignorance as to the true state of Irish affairs. I believe this arose partly from want of correct historical information and partly from a want of that personal knowledge of this country which could only be obtained by a residence in it . . .' Cusack pointed to one illustration of the consequences of such ignorance when it was allied with the habitual presumption that what prevailed in England also existed in Ireland, and to a similar degree: 'English gentlemen naturally suppose that the Irish peasant, or small farmer, has the social advantages of the Englishman of his class, hence they cannot possibly understand one-half of the causes which contribute to make Ireland poor and discontented.' This mixture of ignorance and presumption might not have been so divisive and dangerous had the Irish recognized its existence, but they did not. Cusack remarked that the Irish patriot 'does not always give his English friends credit for their ignorance, nor probably . . . will he understand it'. Some of this ignorance was deliberate, in the sense that Englishmen, like any other people, were adept at avoiding the contemplation of unpleasantness and failure. But the Irish nationalist view, assuming knowledge where it did not exist, neglected education in favour of an aggressive berating, and saw malice where the reality was often ignorance and neglect.

Once established, images had a coercive power, the power by which life may be compelled to imitate art. The expectation that events and people would conform to images of them sometimes produced precisely that result. Coercion of Irishmen deemed to be terrorists produced terrorists. The swing of Irish public opinion towards support of the 1916 rebellion is often attributed to the way in which England responded to it. It might also be attributed to a reaction against the English depiction of it. The English saw the rebellion as treachery in which all Ireland had conspired. All Ireland had not, but the English determination or willingness to cast Ireland in that role fostered a growing popular enactment of it.

Images bred acceptance of type-cast roles of mutual estrangement from which the actors could never escape: whatever the changes in the empirical situation, Paddys and terrorists would always confront imperialists and landlords because that was the way in which the participants conceived their conflict, thus dooming it to repeat itself in the old ways, and thus reviving all the traditional antipathies. So, the idealized and pure Britain revered by nineteenth-century Protestant Unionists no longer exists, if it ever did. And the Britain reviled by traditional Irish nationalists is changed also — as is the Pope's green island of Paddys and peasants. But these traditional images work still to prevent the emergence of present realities.

A basic problem has been that images derived from situations of conflict perpetuate both the conflict and themselves. The old images breed new conflict which, being interpreted in terms of those images, confirms and sustains them. New events are fed back into the historical continuum thus intensifying the influence both of contemporary events and of their historical precursors. Attempts by politicians to disown traditional images or allow them to become irrelevant are extremely hazardous, as this is seen as betrayal or weakness. Politicians were — and are — expected to live up to popular expectations based on images. In August 1969 Mr Jack Lynch, the Prime Minister of the Irish Republic, made moves and declarations in keeping with the mood of an electorate long fed on images of eventual desirable Irish unity: Mr Chichester Clark, Prime Minister of Northern Ireland, interpreted the disorder which had provoked Lynch's reaction, as a conspiracy of hooliganism manipulated by the Republic in a campaign for unity. Both politicians were aware of the unreality and inadequacy of the images to which they gave lip-service, but they were constrained by the power of tradition. The bigger and more obvious the gap between what really existed and what traditionalists believed ought to exist, the greater was the pressure from such traditionalists to make ideals into reality. The celebration in 1966 of the fiftieth anniversary of the Easter Rebellion drew attention to the distance which separated the Republic from the national ideals of 1916. Reforms in Northern Ireland were seen as departures from the ideal. In both cases, extremists had a firm image of what their ideal was: the question was, to what lengths would they go to achieve or preserve it?

The Union was — or so it seemed to the Irish — a relationship of integration and subordination. This interpretation became immediately operative in Irish consciousness. Ireland became England-orientated. However, the Union, being in origin an expedient, did not produce any similar degree of impact on English consciousness. There was little if any appreciation that the formality of inclusion in the United Kingdom might have altered the status of Ireland as 'other' — subject, and essentially foreign. Thereafter, for

England, the relationship had a conveniently dual complexion: Ireland could be treated as an integral part of England, or as distinct from it, whichever suited prevailing political or economic convenience. The differing Irish and English attitudes towards the Union are readily explicable in terms of the relative dimensions occupied by that arrangement in the affairs of the two countries. It was of paramount significance for Ireland, and of relatively minor importance in the affairs of imperial Britain.

So it was that the Irish regarded the relationship with a consistent seriousness amounting to obsession, while among the English it might provoke casual levity, callous amused contempt, or uncomprehending dismissal. *The Times* could remark in 1846, as famine bit deep into Ireland: 'Without attributing the splendid qualities of the British lion wholly to the agency of beef-steaks, we may pronounce that a people that has been reared on solid edibles will struggle long and hard against the degradation of a poorer subsistence . . . For our own part, we regard the potato blight as a blessing. When the Celts once cease to be potatophagi, they must become carnivorous. With the taste of meats will grow the appetite for them; with the appetite the readiness to earn them.'

In the early 1880s Disraeli put aside Irish discontent with a wave of his hand: 'There! if you say "Bo!" loud enough to a goose—the goose will go away.' The spectacle of the election of the Sinn Feiner, Arthur Griffith, from inside gaol in 1918 moved Ian Hay to enunciate the general principle that 'The redeeming feature of Irish politics lies in the fact that the grimmest tragedy is never far removed from the wildest farce'.

Against such attitudes—whose illustration might be multiplied indefinitely—can be set those English reactions which exhibited genuine concern and benevolence, though here the range of illustration is more limited. A good example is the Marquess of Anglesey, Lord Lieutenant of Ireland in the late 1820s and early 1830s. Anglesey was eventually to resign in disgust with British policy. His sympathy with the Irish is evident in his contention that 'no one can expect a whole population to lie down and starve patiently', but the need to assert such a proposition implies its disregard by others. Anglesey's solution to the Irish question was prompt application of conciliatory paternalism: 'Pat will do what he ought, if justice is done to him, and if the consideration of his miseries is not long delayed.' However, the continuing problem was, that the structure of parliamentary politics frustrated any programme of conciliatory reforms by introducing delays and diminutions. To achieve anything it was necessary to placate the defenders of the *status quo* at the same time as bowing to the need for reform, which was the basis of the frequent association of coercion with conciliation. English ministers took the view that politics was the art of the possible and that the Irish must see and accept that. The possible was bounded by the rights of property, the need to maintain order, the need to take account of vested interests and established institutions , as well as the necessity of proceeding cautiously in complex matters.

There was also the powerful extra factor, peculiar to the Irish situation, of a firmly entrenched Anglo-Irish and Scots Protestant ascendancy, preoccupied with their own self-interests and the maintenance of the *status quo*, and numerically dominant in the British administration of Ireland. In the matter of vested interests, the landlords are most obvious, but up to 1869, the Church of England was possibly just as important, being powerful in the English as well as the Irish establishment, sacred in its claims, and intimately involved with virtually every Irish grievance.

This review of the forces arrayed in defence of the Irish *status quo*, might be taken to imply the suggestion that British governments wished to alter the *status quo* in Ireland, but were prevented from doing so. Quite the contrary. They wished the *status quo* to remain, but were obliged, by the pressure of Irish agitation and disorder, to attempt to adjust the existing structure to ensure its smoother operation. Certainly there were not lacking Englishmen to protest in the English parliament against the coercion of Ireland, but usually this was on the English ground that such coercion contravened the constitution by infringing the rights of the subject — and of course these few critics were always overwhelmed. In those in England who did seek long-term solutions, and genuine reforms rather than stop-gap expedients, paternalism, even self-righteous-ness, was too often apparent. Of most of them might be said what Bryce remarked to Gladstone: 'He had a tendency to persuade himself, quite unconsciously, that the course he desired to take was a course which the public interest required. His acuteness soon found reasons for that course; the warmth of his emotions enforced the reasons. It was a dangerous tendency, but it does not impeach his honesty of purpose.'

The various exigencies of English politics and politicians were one source of trouble. Another was the lack of co-operation between the Dublin administration and the Westminster government. It was occasionally possible — as in the case of the 1831 Arms Bill — for Irish legislation to be introduced into parliament without being seen by either the Dublin administration or, indeed, the British cabinet. The effects of this kind of malfunction can be seen in the 1831 case: the government immediately modified the Bill, but this was too late to avoid an outburst of enraged Irish protest, led by O'Connell. Then there was the fact that initiative in Irish policy lay with Home Secretaries or Chief Secretaries whose interests and abilities (or lack of them) as well as personal attitudes and beliefs, were vital to Irish affairs. Few Home Secretaries were really interested in Ireland. Some, like Lord Melbourne in the early 1830s, were bored by Ireland, angered by its endemic violence, and essentially unwilling to work out any Irish policy. As to the Chief Secretaries, the most powerful centres of British decision-making within Ireland, not many had ability, and in any case their frequent brevity of tenure disrupted continuity: there were nine Chief Secretaries between 1800 and 1812.

The English image of the responsibilities of the Union was, then, a very circumscribed and flickering one. While the Irish lived with the relationship all the time, for it dominated their domestic day-to-day affairs, for England it was an external matter, only occasionally pressing. 'So with all this,' wrote James Callaghan, referring to all the other matters which confronted him as Home Secretary in the winter of 1967–8, 'I had no occasion to seek more work or to go out and look at the problems of Northern Ireland, unless they forced themselves upon me.' However natural, the fact that England attended to Ireland only when it was compelled to, only when there was something patently wrong, had a range of unfortunate effects. It constantly reinforced the image of Ireland as being incurably violent, for violence was taken to be the disease, not merely a symptom. It was violence which attracted the attention of English politicians, it was violence which prompted press reportage, pamphleteering, parliamentary speeches, and, more recently, television coverage.

An image constructed in such circumstances was bound to be controversial, and to create distortion. As the power of the press grew in the second half of the nineteenth century so did controversy over the images it presented. The Tory newspapers gave particular offence to the Irish by way of their editorial comments, but the general content of English reporting and the impressions conveyed have remained under Irish challenge until the present. It has been contended by Eamon McCann that 'the great majority of the British people, dependent on the press to tell them what is happening in the North of Ireland, are by now *incapable* of forming a judgement about it, so one-sided has the reporting been'. Such recent Irish complaint has centred around the attribution of all violence to the Irish Republican Army, and the depiction of the average British soldier as 'a great defender of civilization against chaos, of order against the apostles of violence. He is the most patient, decent, military man in the world'. Neither of these images is recognized as remotely true by such Irishmen as see the IRA as protectors against Protestant and Army violence, and who see the Army as enemies and legalized terrorists: others, less committed, have still been unhappy with the way their understanding of facts has failed to square with such general British imagery.

But it was the extreme images developed in times of violence that tended to endure, and such periods of quiet as there were swiftly dropped out of English consciousness to produce an image of constant turbulence. Ireland's propagandists fostered this by concentrating, for their English audiences, not on the humdrum or the ordinary, but on the spectacular and the dramatic. This publicizing in Britain of Irish crises and discontent had two opposed effects. To some extent, promotion of an image of Irish turbulence was self-defeating. From the English viewpoint, Irish instability appeared most abnormal, hence both contemptible and in need of remedy: the very fact of the existence of this unhappy state of affairs justified tough intervention to restore stability, or at least prevent its further erosion. Against this, parading the condition of Ireland in its most extreme forms did awaken in England if not any widespread sense of guilt, a feeling of some responsibility to heed grievances. Irish advocates were always keen to use the comments of English critics of Irish policies: these existed in substantial quantity,[1] and although such critiques were often made in the context of an opposition scoring points off a government, their party political origins did not reduce their utility. The Irish were particularly adept at using what the British regarded as their greatest virtues as debating points against Irish policy. The turning of the basic principles of liberty and democracy and fair play and humane treatment and the like against Britain was particularly discomforting to English Liberals (J. S. Mill and Gladstone furnish good examples). Such Liberals, pricked by their consciences, and finding endemic Irish violence distasteful, did eventually feel obliged to pay attention. That this tactic was not decisive is largely explained by the fact that so many Englishmen who cherished these large principles would not

[1]. See J. A. Fox, *A Key to The Irish Question. Mainly compiled from the Speeches and Writings of Eminent British Statesmen and Publicists, Past and Present* (London, 1890), and Jeremiah MacVeigh. *Home Rule in A Nutshell. A Pocket Book for Speakers and Electors*(Dublin and London, 1911).

concede that they applied, at least fully, to the particular
situation of Ireland.

But much more than propaganda, or the insistence on
principles, it was Irish violence that captured English
attention. Obviously, the English refusal to attend to
Ireland's problems short of their violent expression fostered
that very violence which the English most deplored, at the
same time as creating a most adverse atmosphere for any
solution. Cardinal Newman remarked in 1881: 'I wish
with all my heart that the cruel injustices which have been
inflicted on the Irish people should be utterly removed —
but I don't think they go the best way to bring this about.'
But what was the best way? Newman did not say. In
theory the best way was some peaceful way. In practice,
the only way in which the Irish could attract serious
attention to grievances crucial to them was by resort
to the threat of violence or its actual use. Even then,
progress was short term. Anglo-Irish relations were
analogous to the story of the leaking roof: when storms
made attention imperative, the climate was against
anything more than temporary repairs; when the weather
cleared, the problem could be forgotten.

Up to the 1860s, only a tiny minority in Ireland — the
Young Irelanders of 1848 — thought outside the Union
framework. Even O'Connell's agitation for repeal was
directed towards qualification of the Union rather than its
abolition. Other agitations — for Catholic emancipation,
abolition of tithes, land reform, disestablishment — were for
reforms within the Union structure. That structure was
accepted, in England, without much thought, as inviolable.
Under it, as Lord John Russell reminded parliament in
1845, Britain had 'engaged to consider Irishmen as we
consider Englishmen': such reminders, once piously
uttered, seemed sufficient proof in themselves that they
were unnecessary. In practice, from the beginning of the
Union, British policy had been a variant on themes of
coercion and conciliation. Later in the century, conciliatory
measures were inspired by a sense of justice or a wish to win
Ireland over, but in the earlier decades, reforms tended to

be grudging surrenders to clamorous demands or intractable facts, concessions for the sake of stability. This was, of course, the style of the great reform of that period, the 1832 Reform Act — a concession to the middle class in order to preserve aristocratic ascendancy; reform on a truly conservative principle, as Lord Grey described it. Coupled with coercion this kind of reform merely agitated Ireland further — as even some Englishmen could see: 'This quick alternation of kicks and kindness . . . is a system that would make the most credulous people distrustful, and the mildest people ferocious', Edward Lytton Bulwer told parliament in 1833.

But English politicians of this period cared little for Ireland, and frequently took little trouble to disguise this. It might be thought that immediately after the famine the magnitude of that disaster would have made Ireland a constant focus for English attention. In fact it has been suggested by Dr. K. T. Hoppen that the reverse occurred: the Liberals of the 1850s ceased even the attempt to understand Irish politics — they simply banished the image of Ireland from their minds: 'Ireland seemed more remote than Italy, and quasi-nationalist agitation close at hand lacked the fragrant excitement of Garibaldian romanticism . . . English Liberals . . . resembled, in their attitude towards Ireland, men who have seen a ghost and hope that if only they turn smartly away the apparition will somehow disappear . . . one of the real mysteries of mid-nineteenth-century politics is that this concrete, and at times pressing, reality was so long ignored by the Liberals.'

Failure to consider the Irish scene was one element which explains why, up to the 1860s, there was an overwhelming assumption in England that the Union was working satisfactorily. Admittedly there had been problems, difficulties and malfunctions in its operation, but in 1861, John Stuart Mill[2] could write confidently: 'There is now next to nothing except the memory of the past, and the

[2] Mill's views on Ireland are analysed at length by E. D. Steele in 'J. S. Mill and the Irish Question: The Principles of Political Economy, 1848-1865', *The Historical Journal*, xiii, 2, 1970. pp. 216-36, and 'J. S. Mill and the Irish Question: Reform, and the Integrity of the Empire, 1865-1870', *Ibid.* xiii, 3, 1970, pp. 419-50.

difference in the predominant religion, to keep apart the two races . . . The consciousness of being at last treated not only with equal justice but with equal consideration, is making such rapid way in the Irish nation, as to be wearing off all feelings that could make them insensible to the benefits which . . . must necessarily derive from being fellow citizens . . .'

The memory of the past, and the difference in the predominant religion were to remain crucial divisive matters, and Mill's placing of them in a dismissory context indicates that he shared the prevailing English inability to assess their strength. But, quite aside from Mill's gross undervaluing of historical and religious factors, his sanguine estimate of the mood in Ireland was superficial and erroneous: the Irish image of the Union was quite other than what Mill thought, as he was later to recognize.

That Irish image was, from the 1840s, both dominated and epitomized by the famine, a catastrophe that did enormous (and, it could be argued, ultimately fatal) damage to the Union relationship. It provided Irish nationalists with material for a most fundamental and emotional indictment of England—the charge that it contrived the extermination and banishment of the Irish on the scale of mass murder. The reality was that the famine revealed the blind rigidities of English policy and the gross inadequacy of English economic orthodoxy, the doctrine of *laissez-faire*: even more was it simply a disaster beyond all expectation and imagination. But the image which grew, fed by these grievous shortcomings, was one of genocide: '. . . that million and a half men, women, and children, were carefully, prudently, and peacefully *slain* by the English government'—this was to be an enduring nationalist theme, voiced most bitterly and most vehemently in the widely popular histories of John Mitchel. That the nationalist image of the famine was manufactured, not spontaneous, is suggested by the prevalence of the folk-image that it was a punishment of God, but it was a period so terrible, so utterly and profoundly destructive, that no government, even one much more active with remedies than the English, could have avoided being held responsible.

In addition, the famine made the matter of Irish emigration an issue of the most bitter contention. Emigration had been taking place heavily enough for half a century before the famine, but its enormous increase, in the context of starvation, made it an enduring grievance against England. In the English view, Irish emigration was a natural and desirable process, relieving Ireland's problems and greatly benefiting the Irish who left, given the enhanced quality of their new lives elsewhere. In sharp contrast, the Irish nationalist image was one of an in-human depopulation, deliberately fostered by England to suit her purposes of exploitation and domination, an image of agony and distress, of families torn apart, of lives spoiled, of morals degraded — and all because of England: it was a monstrous continuing eviction of a nation contrived by the English. At the same time — or at least by the 1880s — many Irish publicists, particularly politicians and clerics, made a virtue of necessity and took pride in the dispersion of the Irish all over the world, acclaiming this as living proof of the enterprise, industry, and moral greatness of the Irish race. The Irish were able to make of emigration both a massive grievance and a continuing bolster to the national ego, and both these images, negative and positive, had a clear anti-English, anti-Union aspect.

However, the famine and emigration were by no means the only evidence to the Irish that the Union worked against them. Catholic emancipation, envisaged by Pitt in 1800 as a vital part of the Union arrangements, was at last extorted from a reluctant England in 1829, under the duress of powerful agitation. Repeal was denied in such a way as to make clear the coercive realities of union. Land tenure reform was resisted in all essentials. Any concessions prior to the 1860s were minimal, and made for reasons of expediency.

Central to explaining English attitudes to Irish demands within the Union was the conviction that the condition and disposition of Ireland instanced ingratitude. On an English view, which *The Times* at least could sustain even during the famine, England had been generous to Ireland. This conviction keeps obtruding through the history of the Union, sometimes coupled with acknowledgement of past dereliction — but if mistakes had perhaps been made in the past, the present was another, beneficent story.

The Irish image of British treatment was very different. In 1867 J.F. Maguire described it in its American manifestation: ' . . . the profound belief, which lies at the very root of this hostility, and gives life to every anti-British organization — that Ireland is oppressed and impoverished by England; that England hates the Irish race, and would exterminate them, were it in her power . . .' In its particulars, Maguire's plea for a revolution in English attitudes reveals directly and by implication how ugly was the face of England even as it appeared to a moderate Irish reformist: Maguire was no republican:

'Let a generous, kindly, and sympathetic spirit breathe in the language of her statesmen and her orators, and mark the writings of her journalists. Let there be an end, not to say of abuse or denunciation, but of that tone of offensive superiority and still more offensive toleration and condescension which too often characterizes British references to Ireland and things Irish. Let it be the honest, earnest desire of the English people to lift Ireland up to her own level of prosperity and contentment; and obliterate, by generous consideration for the wants of her people, the bitter memories and lurking hate which the wrongs of centuries have left in the Irish heart, and which the apathy and neglect of recent times has taken little trouble to recognize.'[3]

[3] The continued sensitivity of the Irish to what they regard as an English 'tone of offensive superiority . . . and condescension' is illustrated by the strong Irish resentment occasioned by Edward Norman's *A History of Modern Ireland* when it was published in 1971. This book emphasized the positive and constructive contribution which English government made to Irish affairs and development under the Union, but this line of argument, however historically interesting and useful as a counterbalance to nationalist interpretations, is not one popular in an Ireland where little good has been discerned in English rule. Moreover, Dr Norman tended to diminish and make fun of movements and men taken very seriously by the Irish and regarded by them as important in their history as a

England's belief that its conduct towards Ireland was beneficent and merited gratitude was based on the belief that England had no obligation to recognize Ireland's claims, which were normally excessive or visionary, and that to attend to them at all was *ex gratia*. Palmerston explained the slight limitation on landlord's powers proposed in his abortive 1855 Irish Land Bill as 'bad enough though excusable in consideration of the peculiar circumstances of the country', the implication being that England endured such evils in Ireland's interests. Concessions were always minimal because, at least in the earlier decades of the nineteenth century, English governments believed that they had infallible political formulas (proved in England) for achieving stable prosperous government. These formulas consisted—to take the definition of Lord Grey's ministry—of the maintenance of order at all costs plus remedial measures to remove laws obnoxious to the Irish people. Perfect in conception, such formulas were radically vitiated by their restriction within the confines of scared English property rights, and by simple inertia. Yet such was the faith of English politicians in the infallibility of their formulas that they were often surprised, and sometimes distressed, to find that what remedies they tendered failed to please the Irish. The failure was, at least partly, a consequence of the limitations of the Whig, and later Liberal, conception of liberty. This conception was largely restricted to the idea of extending civil liberties by removing restrictions and abuses and inequities: it did not extend to economic intervention or to the positive legislative programme of reform which Ireland needed. Thus, at the

people. His book, therefore, may be seen as a good example of a modern 'English' interpretation of Irish history—'English' in the sense of being experienced by the Irish as offensive, and embodying qualities they have traditionally associated with English appraisals of their affairs. There are numerous examples of such English interpretations in the nineteenth century. Some twentieth-century books whose titles indicate English imagery are T. W. H. Crosland, *The Wild Irishman* (London, 1905). ('The pathriot is singularly and peculiarly Irish. There is nothing like him in England, and there will never be anything like him; for he comes like water and like the wind he goes', p. 41); J. Chartres Molony, *Ireland's Tragic Comedians* (London, 1934) under which title is discussed, not the Irish stage, but a number of Irish patriots, including Wolfe Tone and Robert Emmet; and the Earl of Middleton, *Ireland—Dupe or Heroine* (London, 1932).

beginning of the violent and widespread tithe war of the 1830s, the Home Secretary considered reform of grand juries to be the most urgent Irish problem. While Ireland lapsed into rural crisis and agrarian outrage, the government addressed itself to peripherals until the turmoil forced its attention to the central problem—to which its major response was that of coercion.

The fact that English governments saw Ireland's problems as existing in areas quite different from those which actually agitated the Irish led to frustration and fury on both sides. To take the English view, Irish behaviour was deplorable, irrational, and provocative, and such was the continued and quite unjustified state of unrest, obstruction, and atrocity, that it was to England's credit that she did not handle Ireland much more sternly: she had shown restraint where harshness would have been completely excusable.

The conviction that England had treated Ireland magnanimously was particularly evident as England began to take Irish reform more seriously. In November 1869 the English press was astonished that, in view of the generosity of proposed legislation, an Irish electorate should elect the Fenian O'Donovan Rossa. *The Times* took this revival of the Fenian spirit to be 'without any visible cause or favouring circumstances' and confessed itself baffled by 'one of those Irish paradoxes which Englishmen find it hard to understand'. There was a similar response to the Irish elections of 1874 which ousted Gladstone's Liberals and returned fifty-nine Home Rule supporters. This was greeted not as a significant adverse reaction to previous British policy, but rather as a flagrant and unpardonable expression of ingratitude to Gladstone, who had done so much to gain concessions for Ireland. It was construed as typical Irish perversity and stupidity, rather than symptomatic of any genuine impulse.

This judgement was related to other characteristic English estimates of the liberality of the concessions made to Ireland. There was the habit of equating individual political intentions with parliamentary achievement: the Land Act of 1870 was a much lesser measure than

Gladstone's original Bill, but somehow the impression in England was that the Irish had been given all they needed (and to considerable English cost), if not all they said they wanted. There was a tendency to take satisfaction in good intentions — and a generous disposition, rather than its legislative expression, sometimes seemed beneficence enough, especially when Ireland was quiet. After all, as General Smuts reported to the British cabinet in July 1921, the Irish were 'people you can satisfy with phrases'. Some Englishmen could see further. Lord Hartington remarked in 1871: 'No one but a fool could have supposed that the disestablishment of a Church, or the alteration of the position of the stronger tenants by the Act of 1870 would prevent village ruffians from committing outrages.' Such discernment was somewhat flawed by the reduction of Irish agrarian unrest to the activities of village ruffians, but even this degree of insight (or despair) was uncommon. Gladstone took the view in 1871 — at least publicly — that University education for Catholics was the only remaining Irish grievance: certainly he expected that his reforms would usher in a new era of peace and good will. Not only were English politicians guilty of optimism to the degree of self-delusion, but the normal devices of politics pointed in that direction: governments were forever claiming that Ireland was in, or about to enter, a state of peace and tranquillity, and that whatever happened to be the government's current Irish policy was paramount in achieving that.

Another habit of the English political mind was that of refusing, at least initially, to take Irish demands at all seriously. So it was with Home Rule in 1874, widely dismissed by British press and politicians as being silly and quite out of any practical question. When attention to such Irish 'nonsense' became unavoidable, the tendency was to suppose that to give much less than what was asked (that being preposterous) was adequate settlement. In August 1921 Lloyd George, in replying to de Valera, complained: 'The British Government have offered Ireland all that O'Connell and Thomas Davis asked and more, and we are met only by an unqualified demand that we should recognize Ireland as a foreign power.'

Faced with continual Irish demands, the English did accept some blame. Conservatives in particular ascribed Irish unrest to English weakness or indecision, especially to attempts to placate the Irish with concessions. In 1866 the *Pall Mall Gazette* was furious with such English radicals as paid attention to Irish opinions on land tenure: 'If there had been no *Spectator* and no Mr Mill to vitalize their errors by . . . sanctioning them, they might possibly have been greatly weakened, if not extinguished, long ere now.' In the 1880s one of Lord Salisbury's favourite arguments was that the only real danger to the Union was the willingness of weak and sentimental Liberals to consider the wild proposals of a few disloyal and irresponsible Irish fanatics. All would be well with Ireland, conservatives believed, if only Englishmen took a firm and united line. The conclusion to be drawn on the basis of this approach to the Irish question was obvious—the equivalent of the 'no nonsense from the natives, send a gunboat' approach, which was one strand in the tradition of imperialism.

However, especially prior to 1870, England had a perfect scapegoat on which to lay blame for the major problems of Anglo-Irish relations—the owners of land in Ireland, and their agents. Around these, from the early days of the Union, developed a most unfavourable image, that of irresponsible exploiters whose greed and inhumanity prejudiced and undermined all good relations between Ireland and England. Here at least was one image which Irish peasants and English politicians held in common, though from opposite viewpoints. As Irish Chief Secretary 1812-18, Robert Peel was convinced that the major root cause of Irish unrest was the absence of proper local leadership. He believed that the natural leaders of Irish society—that is, the owners of the land—must be induced to discharge their appropriate role and duties, those of firm paternalism, and then the Irish problem would largely solve itself. This—an assessment based on an interpretation of how English society worked—proved an enduring English conviction: social disturbance in Ireland flowed from the abdication of leadership by the landowning class. So, during the famine, both its causes and its relief were held in Britain to be the responsibility of Irish landowners. The unwelcome surge of Irish migration to Britain in the 1830s and thereafter was attributed to the iniquity and malpractice of Irish landowners, who drove out paupers whose care was their responsibility. A similar theme runs through J.S. Mill's *Principles of Political Economy*: in editions from 1848 to 1865, Mill blamed landlords for the condition of Ireland, depicted them as having abused their rights, and traced all rural unrest to their economic oppression.

This was a superficial interpretation, distracting attention away from the real problems—those of a primitive and ailing economy, and of the social consequences of animus and hatred that went back to the earliest English conquests and confiscations. But it was an explanation which suited English attitudes, in that it placed the fault externally, and not at the heart of English policies.

In view of such attitudes, it is easy to see why the relationship between England and Ireland has often been regarded as colonial: Ireland was England's 'colonial laboratory' in which, at the beginning, the future pattern of British colonization was set, and at the end, the classic pattern of decolonization was established. This interpretation might excuse English misunderstanding and mismanagement. Here was a new situation in which, naturally, mistakes were made and lessons learnt for the future. It is true that the situation in Ireland exhibited some classically colonial features. Visiting Ireland in 1856, Engels discerned a colonial situation in the large numbers of 'gendarmes' he encountered: he had never seen so many in any country. And one extreme strand in the Irish reaction perhaps goes as far as the 'mad fury . . . bitterness and spleen . . . ever-present desire to kill us' which Jean-Paul Sartre saw as leaping out of the Third World of Fritz Fanon's *The Wretched of the Earth*. English policy was often squarely in the harshest imperial tradition: to quote Lord Salisbury in 1872: 'Ireland must be kept, like India, at all hazards: by persuasion if possible; if not, by force.' And it was an historical fact that parts of Ireland had been colonized from England and Scotland in the seventeenth and earlier centuries.

Yet Englishmen did not have, in the nineteenth century, a simple colonial image of Ireland. Nor could they be induced to adopt one, for the health of the relationship. Efforts to persuade the English government to apply to Irish land questions policies pursued in India met with firm resistance. J.S. Mill remarked on the presumption behind English policy: 'What was not too bad for us in England, must be good enough for Ireland or if not, Ireland or the nature of things was alone in fault.' In 1867 Isaac Butt pointed to the basic reason for this. He lamented that the principles of Indian land policy were not applied to Ireland 'just because we have the fiction of an identity with England'. This was a genuine and deep-rooted dichotomy in the English image of Ireland. When force was necessary it was used as it might have been in a typically colonial situation, but in matters of policy, the English did not view the Irish as sufficiently different or remote as to necessitate radical departures from English norms. After all, the Irish were white, usually spoke English, lived next door so to speak, and were substantially represented in the British parliament. They were also, through the emigration process, colonists with the British, of the English-speaking world. The Union was a true union to the extent that it bred an attitude of English mind which refused to accept that Ireland might be anything more than a distinctive region within the realm.

There are other important elements of complexity—if not confusion and contradiction—in the English image of Ireland. The fact that Irish affairs so often raised general principles of social, economic, and political change meant that, from early in the Union, questions of Irish reform became entangled with various radical challenges to the English *status quo*, from Chartism to the Labour party. Involvement with the Liberal party meant not only linkage with its fortunes, but sharing the image which conservatives attempted to foister on that party. The Tory reaction, from the 1880s, to the decadent Liberals who had corrupted English life and who sought to undermine its traditional hierarchies was of decisive importance for the future of Ireland. This image of the Liberals was energetically promoted by Ulster Unionists. The Liberal social programme was generally anathema to Unionists who blamed Liberal land legislation in Ireland for undermining British rule there 'by ruining and expelling the gentry'. And when the Liberals undertook in 1911 to curb the powers of the House of Lords, the Tory depiction of them as revolutionaries, subverters of the constitution, reached its most intense form. To an Irish nationalist image, bad enough in its own right among conservatives, was added the imagery of radicalism and revolution generated from within the English scene by changes and challenges occurring there.

As might be expected, resistance to suggestions for reform in Ireland sprang from every source of conservative impulse. Precedent remained a salient argument. Queen Victoria was far from the only one who was afraid that concessions to Irish 'vandalism' would set dangerous precedents in England. However, the conservative response was often much more primitive. It was often proferred as argument enough that as such and such a proposed Irish policy was irrelevant to England, or was not followed there, there was no need for it in Ireland: the fact that it was not done in England was reason enough for not doing it in Ireland. Here was the spirit of true union carried to the degree of absurdity and selfish contradiction.

It has been suggested earlier that English consciousness of the relationship with Ireland fluctuated sharply in keeping with the pressure of Irish events. Violence provoked anger; quiet produced occasional expressions of smug complacency regarding wise English policies, but more usually a simple termination of any English attention at all. But an adverse development in the English image of Ireland can certainly be discerned by the 1870s. The cartoon depiction of the Irishman had moved firmly away from that of the amiable if contemptible peasant buffoon towards that of the dangerous terrorist ape-man. This transformation, reflecting a change in public mood, was wrought by an increasingly adverse experience of the Irish—as immigrants, as the perpetrators of chronic agrarian outrage in Ireland, and as violent enemies of society—Fenians—in England. The simianizing of the Irish cartoon image was linked to the popularization of Darwinian theories, and expressed the English view of the Irish as at a primitive stage in the evolution of man. It also signified that bemused contempt and irritation were being accompanied by growing fear and hatred. In particular, Fenian activity, especially within Britain itself, in the late 1860s, confirmed the presence of the dangerous beast which lurked within the Irish character: the pig was joined by the ape as representing what Englishmen thought of the Irishman's animal behaviour.

At the same time, an additional image was necessary to reflect another dimension of England's attitudes towards Ireland. This was 'Hibernia', the beautiful female personification of Ireland that appears so often in *Punch* and elsewhere, usually beset by simian terrorists, but protected by a stalwart John Bull. This female symbol represented what Englishmen thought Ireland ought to be. Femininity conveyed those soft, poetical, emotional characteristics the English discerned in the Irish, as well as containing the notion of appropriate dependence. Here was noble, warm-hearted, suffering Ireland, reliant on her strong English protector. A picture of Ireland totally given over to violently anti-English terrorists was unacceptable to the English imagination: there had to be a positive rather than a brutally negative moral justification for the English presence, and that was posited to be the defence of the true Ireland, beautiful and rich in spirit, against those forces which sought to degrade her. This English image chimed in with the female-personified Ireland of ancient Gaelic literary tradition, and later in the nineteenth century, the personification became common in Ireland itself. It is impossible to be precise about the effects of male and female images — 'John Bull' and 'Hibernia' or 'Erin' — on Anglo-Irish relations. However, in an England where male and female attributes were categorized and assumed to be so distinct, and where the female was regarded as naturally subject and dependent, the existence of such imagery may not be irrelevant to the unliberated condition of Ireland.

The eruption of Fenian violence in England in 1867, and the existence of Fenian organizations within England and Scotland, represented in the eyes of Victorian England a threat compounded of Ireland, Romanism, republicanism, and mob anarchy: Fenianism seemed to threaten, with popular unrest, the whole social edifice the English middle classes had built. The reaction was extreme. Following the Fenian explosion at Clerkenwell in December 1867, the American minister in Britain reported home: 'It may be doubted whether at any time since the discovery of the scheme of Guy Fawkes there has been so much panic spread . . . throughout this community as at this time . . .' On the surface, 'fenian fever' in Britain was short-lived, but the shock greatly deepened hostility towards the Irish and their claims.

The upsurge of Fenian violence had been preceded by one of those recurrent periods in which the English view was that all was well with Ireland. When Fenian activity first shattered this complacency, the initial press reactions tended to be those of anger at ingratitude, the contention that the whole business was American inspired, not Irish, and general incomprehension that some Irish should be so foolish as not to see the great benefits of the English connection. In November 1865 *The Times* explained the position thus: 'Ireland by being associated with England has obtained a very much better government than she would have had, had she been left to herself . . . [However] It was not in the power of England to force the Irish to trust one another, or to practice in their own country, at least, that steady and persevering industry which has raised England to her present position. Therefore, though extremely well governed, Ireland is not happy or prosperous . . .'

It was shocking, given the excellence of English government, and the fact that Ireland had been presumed calm, that Ireland should resort to violence.

The violence itself was shocking. It jarred harshly against the English belief that Britain, and the British way of life, were paragons of law and order to which violence was quite alien. This belief (or illusion) conditioned not only the way Irish violence was received, but the judgement of the way Britain responded to that violence; that response was assessed on very different criteria, for it was assumed that force, as it emanated from Britain, was always reluctant, restrained, and justified, whereas Irish violence was everything opposite to that.

And Fenianism shocked and outraged England because it dared to bring Irish violence, hitherto a remote phenomenon, into Britain itself. In September 1971 Enoch Powell complained that 'The public in Great Britain are invited to regard Ulster as, in famous phrase, "a far away country of which we know nothing" . . . The third person instead of the first is too often in use to refer to the inhabitants of this province. "Let *them* settle *their* difficulties among themselves" runs the frequent ejaculation, among educated as well as uneducated'. This attitude, in which Ireland was regarded as substantially apart and foreign, was the reverse of the true union coin. The wish that a distressful Ireland would go away, often produced in English minds the illusion, or pretence, that it had, or at least the feeling that Ireland was a very distant place. The disposition to regard it as being far away — geographically — stems from the tacit recognition that it was a country very different from England, plus a reaction to its constantly troublesome behaviour. This produced a wish to be disassociated from it, as a respectable man might wish to avoid, or pretend not to know, a relation whose habits were embarrassing or criminal: Ireland was, colloquially and usually actually, bad news. For some Englishmen — Gladstone being one — a prime compulsion for attending to Ireland was the damage its condition did to England's European and international reputation and prestige. For others, the condition of Ireland was reason for trying to forget it.

Undoubtedly, at times the image of Ireland became so faint in the English mind that it disappeared entirely from consciousness, or was present only as a matter for boredom. No more remarkable instance of this happening was from the end of 1918 to the middle of 1920, when crisis in Ireland itself was at its height. The explanations are obvious — war-weariness, concern with other domestic and foreign issues, and the repellent sameness of the Irish situation. At that time, public apathy about Ireland had some important repercussions. It meant that the situation was left to the politicians to solve, but the politicians were no more enthusiastic than the public, and felt that any vigorous policy would not command public support. So, the government refused to allow the strong coercive policy wanted by the British Army in Ireland — and thus, it might be argued, allowed the Irish situation to drift into one impossible to handle or contain: Britain abandoned violence in Ireland to its own momentum.

The wish that Ireland could sink beneath the sea was not new in 1920-21. In the 1880s there was, Dr E. D. Steele observes, a 'widespread sentiment that England had nothing to lose and much to gain by loosening her ties with Ireland'. The problem was then, as it is now, how could this be managed without damage to England, particularly in the area of prestige. But then another problem existed: from the 1880s, England's political parties were divided over Ireland and any proposed settlement threatened to disrupt most seriously the life of England itself.

Of Anglo-Irish relations following 1921, C.L. Mowat wrote: 'Nothing in the history of the Irish question is so surprising as the suddenness and completeness of its end. It simply disappeared as a major factor in British politics.' As it turned out this fading of Ireland from the English scene was temporary, though the period of vanishment — 56 years — was the longest in the relationship. After 1921, southern Ireland's behaviour did nothing to disturb the traditional image or to question seriously the complacent

English assumption that the settlement of 1920-21 had rid them of the Irish question. After the Anglo-Irish Treaty, those Irish affairs which most attracted the attention of Englishmen were those which appeared to prove just how right they had been about the Irish. There was the civil war, which was taken to show just how violent, barbarous, and utterly irrational the Irish really were. There was Ireland's restlessness as a dominion. Her performance within the British Commonwealth, constantly pushing for power adjustments in favour of dominion autonomy, seemed to prove that the Irish, as traditionally predicted, would try to turn any kind of Home Rule into complete independence. The same conclusion was drawn from de Valera's policies of refusal to accept English claims under the Treaty. Then Irish neutrality during the Second World War appeared to vindicate the English judgement that the Irish were anti-English, ungrateful, and stupidly vindictive. Added to this, the continuance of Irish poverty for so long after independence was taken to confirm the English view of the Irish character as being ineffective and inferior.

Not that Ireland loomed large in English concerns. Depression, international politics, war and its aftermath reduced it by comparison to the smallest importance. It was just that when, occasionally, southern Ireland did obtrude in the English consciousness, it merely confirmed the old images.

Northern Ireland hardly surfaced in English consciousness for opposite reasons: it seemed peaceful, loyal, and stable. Besides, a convention quickly grew up that Westminster did not interfere in Northern Ireland's affairs: soon the situation was that British governments simply did not know what was taking place in Northern Ireland, nor saw any call to attempt to find out.

However, if Ireland vanished from among the major concerns of English politics in 1921, certain images of the English lingered on in Irish minds, both north and south, and these images were to have continuing importance.

In the south, and among nationalists generally, it remained a widespread belief that England was responsible

for the partition of Ireland. For centuries England had
projected in Ireland an image of dominant power and
decisive might. This image was intensified by the imperial
performance and rhetoric of the late nineteenth century—and it was widely accepted (if hated) in Ireland as
a simple fact of life: England's will was law. And, despite
long experience of English party divisions, Ireland tended
to view England as a single entity, at least in the face it
presented to Ireland. Irish nationalists consistently used the
term 'England' to refer to that power against which they
struggled: its Welsh and Scots elements were ignored, or
presumed, because of their Celtic natures, to be
sympathetic to Ireland. There was, in fact, good reason for
believing England to be the centre of resistance to Irish
claims: it was even indicated by election results. The 1886
election saw a majority of Home Rule supporters elected in
Scotland and Wales, but 339 Unionists were elected in the
465 English constituencies. The same was true of the 1892
election, and in 1910 the Liberal majority came from
Ireland, Scotland, and Wales. However, if England was
demonstrably an enemy, there was no strong basis for the
assumption that Wales and Scotland were friends: in
mainland Britain prejudice against the Irish as a people was
most intense in Wales and Scotland, mainly for religious
reasons, and most tenacious there, because these areas bore
the brunt of Irish immigration. But this did not alter the
fact that the Irish believed England to be their foe, and they
commonly invested it with a single, hostile personality.
What followed on this was an assumption that whatever
England decided, particularly within its domestic orbit,
would come about. This assumption took no account of the
bitter political division over how to treat Ireland which
existed in English politics and virtually paralysed all policy
from 1910. To Irish nationalists it was inconceivable that
the Liberals could not cope with Ulster: it must therefore be
that they wanted to admit her objections. It was reported to
the British cabinet in 1920 that this was widely believed in
the south of Ireland, and in 1921 the Irish negotiators made
it clear that they believed that Britain had created the

Ulster difficulty and continued to exploit it. Writing for an Indian audience in 1922, the assistant editor of the *Irish Independent* contended that, if British statesmen had desired, they could have induced Ulster Protestants to accept unity with the rest of Ireland. He interpreted their failure to do so as a further case of Britain's ancient policy of divide and rule, aimed this time at feeding a civil war which would destroy Irish leadership, create anarchy — and thus foster an Irish demand that Britain return.

Suspicion and distrust of England could hardly go further than this — the belief that Britain hoped to re-establish the old Union *via* the use of partition and civil war. In nationalist Ireland, partition was regarded not as the product of the exigencies of politics, or as recognition of the demographic realities, but as another English betrayal. The prevalent assumption had been that Ulster's declaration that it would fight to preserve the Union was mere bluff, but even if it were not, surely English power was sufficient to overcome such resistance?

Undoubtedly, the ultimate reality was that partition was an evasion of the massive and very complex problems posed by and in Ireland's north-east counties, but the immediate reality in 1920-21 was that politics dictated partition. Indeed it might be argued that partition alone made the independence of southern Ireland possible in the circumstances: partition permitted the Irish Free State to come into existence. But the virtually unanimous assumption in the south was, not that partition enabled independence, but that it was a frustration and a withholding of it, a deliberate and arbitrary denial which sustained not only Irish determination to reverse it, but also animus against the power held responsible.

The image which the English retained in Northern Ireland was to prove even more dangerous: again this lay in the realm of automatic assumption. Throughout the Union, as before it, the power of the Protestant ascendancy in Ireland had been based, in the last resort, on the backing of British armed force. This had bred, in that ascendancy, a tendency to exercise power without responsibility, a habit of regarding itself as under the natural protection, should this become necessary, of superior English force. These assumptions and habits of mind continued to prevail in Northern Ireland, while the former need to consider the immediate situation of being a minority within Ireland was removed by their translation into a majority situation in the new state. The government of Northern Ireland retained the assumption that Britain would stand by it, would support it — regardless of its policies — just as it had supported the Protestant ascendancy in the past. In part, this assumption was more an unthinking belief than a reasoned conclusion, but there were also very good reasons for taking that view. From the Ulster Protestant Unionist viewpoint, just as from the Irish nationalist one, Britain was responsible for setting up the partition and the state of Northern Ireland. The Unionists had demanded the continuation of the Union with all of Ireland. Instead they had been given their own government, which they had not sought, together with being confronted on their southern border by a new Irish state they regarded as an enemy. If Britain insisted in putting them in this difficult position, then it was up to Britain to provide protection, not merely for their physical survival but for the continuance of what they regarded as an appropriate society: hence the assumption, which became obvious after 1968, that the internal policies of the province were its own business, and that its own politicians, not the British cabinet, would control such British troops as might be necessary to maintain the existing order. This reliance, misguided as it proved, on unqualified British support for its continued existence, created among Northern Ireland governments an expanded illusion of independence and power. Together with its unbroken majority rule, the image of an ever-present and utterly reliable English support, tempted Northern Ireland governments into the unreflecting continuance of policies long past political tenability.

3

Pride and Prejudice

CENTRAL to the image-making process were matters of mutual pride and prejudice, operative throughout all levels of both societies. At crucial stages, the relationship between England and Ireland demonstrated, just as the recent situation in Northern Ireland has demonstrated, that the real determinants were not amenable to the control of rational politics. As an illustration, the failure of nineteenth-century England to produce reforms large enough and soon enough is paralleled by the similar more recent failure of the Unionist government of Northern Ireland. Some politicians could see the imperative necessity for prompt action; it seems likely that the reforms would have been pacificatory and remedial had they been granted swiftly, but the process was hampered and stifled by the existence of deep-seated and widespread suspicions and prejudices afflicting every level of society. These eroded the will and sapped the political strength of the most discerning politicians, and created, at a grass roots level, an atmosphere which allowed reactionary forces to retard concessions until a degeneration into extremism made them irrelevant. If Ireland was the victim of politics, politics—in that connection—was itself the victim of primitive and irrational prejudices, popular fears, and instinctive hostilities of great depth and power.

On what vision of Ireland and the Irish did the English view of the Union rest? It is a first necessity to appreciate that there was no one unchanging English view. What existed was a group of attitudes and appraisals which, while possessing common and enduring features, were often confused, incoherent, or contradictory, and which fluctuated, from time to time, sometimes wildly, between extremes. To some extent, the English were aware of these inconsistencies in their own assessments, which they explained as being due to the fact that Paddy's character was itself a mass—and a mess—of contradictions. This could produce admission of bewilderment: '. . . his mind is a strange one, and we know not how to deal with it; his creed is equally strange and defies the usual modes of argument. To all men he is a puzzle . . .' More often, the apparent contradictions were taken as being all there was to know: the essence of the Irish was that they were contradictory, unpredictable, irrational, illogical, and best understood as such. Or to sum it all up, as Sir Henry Newbolt did in poetry in 1898, Ireland was mad. The historian H. A. L. Fisher did not go as far. For him in September 1921 only Sinn Fein was mad: Sir Hamar Greenwood, however, thought that all Irishmen had 'strange mental apparatus'. Nor had this condition of English perplexity changed by 1973, as a *Times Literary Supplement* reviewer testified: '. . . exasperation does nothing to remove the bafflement with which the whole problem of Ireland is regarded in this country. On the contrary it enhances it and with wearisome reiteration one is assailed on every side by the all too familiar questions—what do they want, why do they behave like this, what is this murderous doctrine of republican nationalism, why can't the Irish settle their own affairs without involving us.'

Some Irishmen were prepared to concede that Ireland was distracted, perhaps deranged. Roger Casement insisted in 1906 that 'Until the public here in Ireland feel that they *must* tackle the state of their own country and abide by their own acts there can be no real improvement. We have to create a governing mind again after 106 years of abstraction of all mind from this outraged land'. So if Ireland seemed mad, the fault was England's.

No Englishman would accept this, nor did it occur to the typical English mind that Ireland's unintelligibility might be traceable to defects in its own understanding as well as to the abnormality of the Irish. In this regard J.S. Mill's insight was close to being unique: 'Ireland is not an exceptional country but England is. Irish circumstances and Irish ideas as to social and agricultural economy are the general ideas of the human race; it is English circumstances and English ideas that are peculiar. Ireland is in the mainstream of human existence and human feeling and experience; it is England that is in one of the lateral channels.' It was in fact, a basic English postulate that Ireland and the Irish were 'different' in a most exceptional and unacceptable way, 'not influenced by the same feelings as appeared to affect mankind in other countries', as Lord Liverpool put it to Robert Peel in 1816. This theme keeps recurring. Queen Victoria expressed it forcibly in 1867: 'These Irish are really shocking, abominable people—not like any other civilized nation.'

English judgements of the Irish character had direct political implications, not only in suggesting appropriate policies, but in explaining their failure. Why had no remedy been found for Ireland's problems? Because 'Irishmen are not like other people', answered the Conservative minister Hugh Holmes in 1885. Questions of how they differed from other people (notably the English) could lead to quite precise political conclusions. If the Irish were a people afflicted as a Scottish newspaper held in 1849, by 'barbarous spiritual destitution . . . moral and intellectual poverty', then 'vain are grants of money, or the schemes of politicians'. Indeed, were they—as Protestant orators maintained in the famine—the children of anti-Christ upon whom God in order to win them away from the priesthood had sent a scourge, then intervention was not only futile but wrong. If the Irish were an inferior people, bogged in poverty, unable, as it seemed, to produce a professional class, or even skilled workers, then their incapacity for self-improvement demonstrated their inability to govern their own affairs: this must be done for them.

This last conclusion—that England was obliged to govern Ireland because of Irish shortcomings—was very widely held. It tended to coexist with the more positive contention that Ireland was much better off under the Union, indeed that '. . . Ireland, if left to herself, would afford such a spectacle of misery as mankind have never witnessed . . .' as a member told parliament in 1866. Aside from Ireland's political incapacity, it was held in England that it was of benefit to Ireland and to civilization generally if improved and superior nations guided (justly and progressively, of course) the affairs of those less advanced. It was also held, often by the same people, that because of the historical antagonism that existed, an end to the Union would magnify this animus into open enmity, in which Ireland would join England's opponents simply out of its vindictive heart. Moreover, because of its Catholicism, an Ireland unchecked by England would lapse from the fellowship of civilized mankind, because, as J.S. Mill explained in 1868, 'the sympathies . . . of Ireland are sure to be on the same side as the Pope — that is, on the side opposed to modern civilization and progress . . .' So, in retaining the govern- ance of Ireland, the protection of England's immediate interests coincided with her duties of responsibility for the destiny of humanity: to quote Mill again, '. . . the safety, and even the power of England, are valuable to the freedom of the world, and therefore to the greatest and most permanent interests of every civilized people'.

There were, of course, less elevated lines of argument which might be followed from English premises about the nature of the Irish. If Irish unrest sprang from defects in the Irish character and not from English misrule, then there was no point in adjusting the content of English rule, a conclusion indicated also by the fact that when such adjustments were made they produced no lasting pacificatory results. A similar conclusion must be reached if the explanation for the condition of Ireland was geographic or climatic. If as R.A. Macalister wrote in 1935, 'an adverse fluctuation of climate in Ireland must produce physical, moral, and material atrophy', then nothing could be done to change this. Of course, if — as was the Liberal W.H. Duignan's view — 'They are a magnificent race if treated kindly but . . . a very dangerous and unprofitable one to rule with iron', then conciliation was the thing. But if — as was the Tory view — Ireland was a wasteland beyond redemption, and the Irish themselves were incurably violent and responsive only to superior force, then coercion was the only policy. If, as was the opinion of J.A. Froude, the Irish were essentially children, weak and immature, then an adult world must treat them firmly for their own good. To all such denigratory character analysis the Irish tended to reply either with denials in which self-praise was prominent, or by blaming the English for such faults as they acknowledged: these were the inheritance of ages of slavery. If the Irish were not out and out savages, John Denvir claimed in 1892, it was no fault of British rule.

Just as the Irish character presented bafflement and confusion to the English, as well as eliciting an array of dogmatic but conflicting conclusions, so did the Irish question — the problem of what was wrong with Ireland and how it might be remedied. 'I want to see a public man come forward and say what the Irish question is,' Disraeli complained. 'One says it is a physical question; another, a spiritual. Now it is the absence of the aristocracy, then the absence of railroads. It is the Pope one day; potatoes the next.' This classic statement of the condition of the problem has retained its validity down to the present. Debate continues, now focused on the situation in Northern Ireland, as to what really impels the continuing conflict — is it sectarianism, economic deprivation, the clash of nationalisms or cultures, a morbid psychological condition, or what? Whatever the impulses discerned, English assessments tend to come back to a common conclusion, that the whole business was, and is, grossly abnormal.

Historically, this central image of Ireland and the Irish as not conforming to normality had important effects on English policy. When that policy met resistance or failed in its purpose, the immediate assumption was that the fault lay in the people, not in the policy. As any Irish reaction would always be abnormal, irrational, and inexplicable, such reactions could be readily discounted as irrelevant to the merit of policies. What was not realized was that to the

Irish, much of English policy itself seemed abnormal, irrational, and inexplicable because it did not fit the Irish situation as they saw it. Nor would the Irish concede that they had any monopoly on abnormal or discreditable behaviour. Roger Casement would concede that an individual Englishmen might be a gentleman, but collectively, the English were unprincipled and without conscience, 'a most dangerous compound . . . a national type that has no parallel in humanity'.

The tendency for both English and Irish to except the other nation from normal participation in the commonalty of mankind had a seriously weakening effect on their conceptions of what morality might be applicable to such an abnormal relationship. It was an important factor both in canonizing violence in Ireland and in inducing the English to substitute coercion for policy, in order to keep within some bounds what Peel saw in 1813 as 'that natural predilection for outrage and a lawless life which I believe nothing can control'. What was most remarkable, in the context of this English orthodoxy that the Irish were beyond improvement, was that the English continued to ponder and attempt such improvement. In 1829, after long and frustrating experience with and in Ireland, Peel was still seeking 'a system of measures for the permanent civilization' of Ireland. Constantly lamenting the impossibility of their civilizing mission, the English continued to attempt to pursue it.

In part, this can be explained as a consequence of one aspect of the English image of the Irish situation. A favourite theme was that the Irish were an emotional and credulous people, gullible and easily led, who had become the victims of agitators and malcontents. Remove these destructive and corruptive forces and the population would become open to the processes of 'permanent civilization'. But much more important to an explanation is English pride, to which the condition of Ireland offered constant affront. Writing in 1881, under the pessimistic title, 'The Incompatibles', Matthew Arnold advanced a highly optimistic line of reasoning based on the remarkable qualities of the English people: '. . . the English people, with its "ancient and inbred piety, integrity, good nature and good humour", has done considerable things in the world . . . I refuse to believe that such a people is unequal to the task of blending Ireland with itself in the same way that Scotland, Wales and Cornwall are blended with us, if it sets about the task seriously.' The challenge of blending admitted incompatibles was accepted by England because it impinged so intimately and directly on the English self-image, an element of which was the conviction that England could do anything if it really tried. The other side of this coin was an English determination not to be defeated in its objectives by the mere Irish. As time went by without a resolution of her Irish difficulties, the engagement of English pride became more, not less considerable. It was of course possible to take whatever occurred in Ireland as tribute to English virtues. Concessions and reforms were attributed to farseeing magnanimity. Unrest was handled with remarkable tolerance and forebearance, or with resolute adherence to the responsibilities of government and the principles of law and order. It was even possible, at the end, to take pride in the virtue of humility: according to the *Manchester Guardian* in August 1921, by offering Ireland dominion status, England had 'swallowed her pride as few Governments in history'.

Paradoxically, this stubborn confidence that England could solve the Irish question was a major barrier to its doing so, for its natural consequence was a dictated solution rather than a negotiated one, an English solution rather than one jointly achieved. It was also an attitude which bred rigidity and intransigence and righteousness of a kind particularly abrasive to the Irish. Here again emerged the prevailing English conviction, related to imperial concepts of civilizing role and burdens, that England had both a mission and a responsibility towards Ireland. Prior to the full development of the imperial idea in the later nineteenth century, this conviction took the more generalized form of the belief that England had a special role in the progress of humanity because it was, as J.S. Mill explained in 1861 'the

Power, which of all in existence, best understands liberty' and had 'attained to more of conscience and moral principle in its dealings with foreigners than any other great nation . . .'

Not surprisingly, this claim was challenged in Ireland, but it was also part of the self-image which the English projected very powerfully there, so powerfully that some Irishmen accepted it, while those who questioned it took it very seriously, so seriously as to feel the need to urge most strenuously a strong counter-image. In 1900, Canon Sheehan depicted this confrontation in his novel *Luke Delmege*.[1] Delmege, impressed by his experience of England, and disenchanted with Ireland, his home, puts the question to Father Martin, 'Is it not clearly England's destiny to bring all humanity, even the most degraded, into the happy circle of humanity . . .' Martin replies:

'And you really think England has got a Divine mission? I never think of England but as in that dream of Piranesi — vast Gothic halls, machinery, pulleys, and all moving the mighty rolling mechanism that is crushing all the beauty and picturesqueness of the world . . . England's mission is to destroy and corrupt everything she touches —'

'What you call congenital prejudice,' said Father Martin, gravely, 'I call faith. It is our faith that makes us hate and revolt from English methods. To the mind of every true Irishman, England is simply a Frankenstein monster, that for over seven hundred years has been coveting an immortal soul. He has had his way everywhere but in Ireland; therefore he hates us.'

Here was a stance in which England's claims to greatness and superiority were rejected as utterly false and corrupt, while at the same time a contrary set of values was set out in

[1] At least two prominent Irish historians have made substantial use of novels for investigations of Irish social history, K.H. Connell, 'Catholicism and Marriage in the Century following the Famine' in his *Irish Peasant Society. Four Historical Essays* (Oxford, 1968) and Oliver MacDonagh, *The Nineteenth Century Novel and Irish Social History*, O'Donnell Lecture delivered at University College, Cork on April 21 1970 (National University of Ireland, Dublin 1970). To quote Professor MacDonagh (p. 3) the novel 'can yield insights and possibilities of recovering special portions of the past, for which we shall search in vain in any other matter'.

which the Irish excelled: Delmege becomes convinced that 'a race with a priceless history and a present unencumbered with material problems, must have of necessity a rich and glorious future'. So the Irish took pride, and built a conviction of moral superiority, precisely in those things the English saw as their degradation—their religion, their poverty, and their history. In Britain itself the Irish were even capable of idealizing the extreme poverty of their slums, as still preserving the virtuous life. At the same time, they could be effusively proud of worldly success. Successful or distinguished emigrants were celebrated as evidence of the inately superior—or at least equal—qualities and talents of the Irish once removed from the oppressions of Ireland. There was also the claim that, even in its oppressed condition, Ireland embodied a value system and life-style vastly superior to that of England. The contrast is made directly in a social science textbook published in 1932. Rev. E. Cahill contrasted the condition of the nineteenth-century Irish peasant with that of his English counterpart. The Irishman was then 'probably the most oppressed and impoverished human type in Europe'. The English peasant was well-off, free, and the citizen of a great imperial nation. 'Yet, in all the best things of life, domestic happiness, contentment, consciousness of his human dignity, moral and intellectual culture . . . the Irish peasant enjoyed immeasurably the greater share of temporal happiness . . . his advantage in that respect over his English neighbour was due almost entirely to his Catholic faith.' The erection by the Irish of a proud national image on exactly the characteristics most despised by the English—Romanism, poverty, and the rural life—had the effect of rendering incomprehensible to the English, Irish national pride.

All this increased English bewilderment and irritation. No less damaging to the relationship was the effect this particular inflation of the Irish sense of pride had on the Irish themselves. Sean O'Faolain once observed that 'The greatest curse of Ireland . . . has been the exaggeration of Irish virtue—our stubbornness, conservatism, enormous arrogance, our pride of resistance, our capacity for taking punishment, our laughter, endurance, fatalism, devotion to the past, all taken to that point where every human quality can become a vice instead of a virtue'. The growth of a highly idealized self-image was a notable feature of Irish life by the end of the century. It was fiercely antagonistic to West Britons—those Irish who were held to have accepted an English life-style and values—and to the realism of its own artists, as was evident in the storm which raged around the depiction of the Irish peasantry in J.M. Synge's *The Playboy of the Western World* in 1907. The popular Irish self-estimate which developed at this time took great pride both in its distinctive differences from the English and in its sense of its own nobility and purity.

The growth of this self-image had profound effects on the more extreme representatives of the Irish national mind. It produced among them a bitter sense of degradation, at the gap between the ideal and reality, a situation for which they blamed the English—and Irish effeteness. The feeling among these men that, as Padriac Pearse claimed, 'There has been nothing more terrible in Irish history than the failure of the last generation' became particularly intense as the First World War demonstrated the extent to which intransigent Irish nationalism had been weakened. Irish workers had joined the British army, Irish farmers were supplying food to Britain, Irish girls worked in munition factories or hospitals in Britain, the Irish middle class took a British view of the war. All of these realities were shameful departures from the ideal—which the idealists determined to reassert at Easter 1916.

It would be impossible to assess to what extent England's self-estimate, and its estimate and treatment of the Irish, actually created Irish nationalism by way of reaction, but there can be little doubt that these things greatly fostered it. As it developed in the nineteenth century, Irish nationalism took on a distinctive character whose elements were the shared experience and convictions of the majority of Irishmen in relation to history, culture and language. religion, and land—and antagonism to English rule. These

points of distinctive reference gradually hardened into a
nationalist stereotype which not only rejected things
English, but was intolerant of such things Irish as did not
measure up to all its requirements. Most of this intolerance
it vented on those Irishmen whose characteristics conformed
to the stereotype but who refused or neglected to take up an
aggressive or extreme nationalist position. But what of those
in Ireland who did not conform to the features of the
stereotype?

Irish nationalists were obsessed with achieving unity (they
were 'unity-mad' Michael Davitt once complained) to the
degree where they simply refused to acknowledge — or even
note — that the existence of Ulster Unionism demonstrated
that unity, in terms of the stereotype, did not exist. This obsession may be traced to what was seen and felt among
nationalists as the sheer enormity of their task: they proposed to extort their freedom, and recognition of their
identity, from the greatest imperial power in the world,
which dwarfed them in terms of population, wealth, resources, and military might, and which projected outwards
the image of immense self-confidence and conviction of
superiority. In such circumstances of inferiority, unity
among the challengers was an absolute first necessity. Without it, any form of nationalist demand would be gravely
weakened and any moral case jeopardized. If unity did not
exist, then it had to be invented.

It is often forgotten that the 1916 rebellion was very
much part of this process of invention. At the time, that
rebellion was 'universally and explosively unpopular'. Those
who planned it were very clearly aware that national unity
as they desired it simply did not exist. Conscious that they
were very much a minority among those who possessed the
attributes of the nationalist stereotype, they conceived their
first and major duty as that of arousing that majority. So
large was that problem, so immediate and so familiar, that
it is perhaps not surprising that they regarded it as virtually
their only problem, quite neglecting the profound difficulty
posed by the remote and unfamiliar Ulster Protestant
world. Tactics and self-image, as well as a calculation of

priorities, encouraged the same neglect. Unity was imperative if the English were to be confronted effectively, and the most dynamic nationalist image did not admit of any exception to a united Ireland desiring to control its own affairs. In the classic revolutionary tradition, Irish extremists claimed to be acting in the best interests, and to represent the real desires, of all Irishmen. Whatever the majority might think at the moment, once the extremists had acted towards achieving the real will of the nation, all would be changed, changed utterly. If there appeared to be a flaw in the seamless robe of nationhood, then this was either unreal, a delusion, or was being artificially manufactured: it would vanish in the process of achieving nationhood. Seen in this perspective the situation in Ulster presented no greater a difficulty to nationalists than that of enlisting the support of an apathetic or antagonistic majority in the south. Nationalists were not, as has been recently insisted, 'blind' to the Ulster difficulty. Many of them appreciated Ulster's distinctive character as being of great antiquity, related to the geographic fact that this was the area closest to mainland Britain. But they regarded this as a provincial difference which would exist happily within the nation. The fact that this difference was proclaimed belligerently within Ulster as utterly irreconcilable with any proposal of Irish nationhood could be explained to nationalist satisfaction. A favoured interpretation of Ulster's apparent intransigence was that English and Protestant Irish Tories had inflated and exploited religious divisions to suit their own interests. This explanation had sufficient validity to foster the illusion that the entirety of divisive sectarianism was artificial and would disappear once its stimulus was removed under Home Rule. It was also a common nationalist belief that however alien might be the atmosphere and disposition of Belfast city, Irish nationalism in the north—the true Ulster spirit—was all the more intense because of this, and all the more certain to triumph over difficulties.

This superficial approach, promoted, even in Britain, simple attitudes towards resolving the Irish question, until

Protestant Ulster drew attention to the basic complexities in the most assertive and uncompromising way. It is a curious fact that Protestant Ulster went on to adopt a similar convenient illusion: from its formation, the Northern Ireland government subscribed to a kindred wholist myth, that it was a Protestant state, an approach which virtually ignored the disagreeable existence of half a million awkward Catholics within its borders.

The issue of Home Rule versus Unionism, particularly in relation to the question of Ulster, presents some outstanding examples of the power of images to determine the course of Anglo-Irish relations. It illustrates their deliberate exploitation, their capacity to blind and deceive, and their tendency in a situation of conflict to worsen the situation and to deepen antagonisms.

Certainly Irish nationalists had a gravely defective appreciation of the nature of Protestant Unionist opposition to Home Rule.[2] Parnell expressed their common assumption: 'Protestants, other than the owners of land, are not really opposed to the concession of a full measure of autonomy to Ireland.' A few landlords and religious bigots were making protest noises, but Ulster was sound at heart and needed no special attention. Such wishful nationalist thinking was dangerous, but among English politicians its repercussions were more serious still, for theirs was the ultimate responsibility. If Irish nationalists ignored the feelings of Ulster Unionists, so also did English politicians. In 1893 Gladstone infuriated a deputation of prominent Ulster Unionists by treating them, and their case, with virtual contempt: Orangemen concluded that he was 'a self-seeking and reckless old politician abetted by a motley and

---

[2] For Irish Unionism, see the following, all by Patrick Buckland; *Irish Unionism: One. The Anglo-Irish and the New Ireland 1885-1922* (Dublin, 1972); *Irish Unionism: Two. Ulster Unionism and the Origins of Northern Ireland 1886-1922.* (Dublin, 1973), *Irish Unionism 1885-1923. A Documentary History* (Belfast 1973); *Irish Unionism* (The Historical Association Pamphlets 81, London, 1973).

For the period after 1922 and the Ulster Unionist Party in particular, see John Harbinson, *The Ulster Unionist Party, 1882-1973* (Belfast, 1973).

For the atmosphere of Ulster Unionism, see Ernest Hamilton, *The Soul of Ulster* (London, 1917) and James Winder Good, *Ulster and Ireland* (Dublin, 1919)

heterogeneous rabble of professional agitators'. Gladstone's reaction stems perhaps from his age, and virtual obsession with Home Rule, but the general English tendency to ignore Ulster objections or not treat them seriously, sprang from the habit of not responding to Irish claims unless under extreme pressure — and up to 1910 that had come only from advocates of Home Rule.

What is more, the English political imagination could not encompass the possibility that persons who were obviously conservatives and loyalists might take their objections to extreme lengths: Irish nationalists held a monopoly of the revolutionary image. So, however vocally Ulster Unionists might object to Home Rule, in the end their conservatism and loyalty would compel them to accept it. So ran English political logic, and therefore Unionist threats could be safely ignored or perhaps humoured a little. Indeed, on the matter of the firmness of Ulster's purpose, English political perception was substantially inferior to that of some Irish nationalists, defective though that was itself. By 1893 Irish members were telling the House of Commons that the Ulster party was a revolutionary party, but no one believed them: that claim seemed altogether absurd, and parliament accepted without question the Unionist depiction of themselves as the constitution's most loyal defenders.

Only in one regard were some English Liberal politicians and Irish nationalists willing to take the Ulster situation seriously. The recurrence of sectarian disturbances in Ulster was used as an argument to support Home Rule. Riots were depicted as the consequence of oppression by a bigoted Unionist minority that sought to silence the rightful demands of the majority for Home Rule. Sectarian strife was taken not as evidence that Home Rule was not wanted, or would be rejected, but as proof of its greater necessity.

Ulster Unionists, seeing themselves and their stand appraised in England as being of little account, took the lesson that they must make themselves of account. They must exert on England pressure in excess of that exerted by nationalists, as this was evidently the only way in which they could hope to gain attention. Thus, the English misunderstanding and undervaluing of the Ulster question led to its becoming much more aggressive and uncompromising in its expression. To Ulster Unionists, English attitudes seemed to demand that Ulster project an image both more menacing and more attractive than did the Home Rule movement. From 1908 they mounted a very thorough propaganda campaign in Britain to achieve these objects. It was a campaign which, together with events in Ireland, had considerable effect, not least on Unionists themselves, for it hardened their own outlook in the process: by 1912, when the Liberal government was not unwilling to make special provision for Ulster, Unionists hardly bothered to consider such compromise, so insistent had they become on the complete abandonment of Home Rule for any part of Ireland.

The positive aspect of the Ulster Unionist campaign was to depict themselves as utterly loyal defenders of the constitution and of the British way of life. They claimed that they embodied all the British virtues and sought to preserve Britain from developments inimical to her true interests. However, the negative aspect of the campaign was much more prominent, for Unionists saw their best chances in blackening the image of Home Rule.

Having been subjected to the assumption that their Unionism need not be taken seriously, they sought to exhibit Home Rule in a similar light. They asserted that it had no valid factual basis: Ireland had never been a separate nation in the past, and claims for its distinctive culture were fictitious or exaggerated. They insisted that the English connection was vital to what civilization and prosperity Ireland possessed. They denied that the Irish people wanted Home Rule. Such as said they did, or who voted for Home Rule candidates, did so because they were either deluded or intimidated by a tiny disaffected minority of priests and agitators. When, later, Sinn Fein entered the public arena, a similar tactic was applied to it: witness Ernest Hamilton's explanation:

'The organization was originally started by a few ecstatic

cranks whose aim was the revival of bombastic native poetry, and of ancient dresses which had never existed . . . A fruitful recruiting ground was soon found among hooligans, corner-boys and loafers generally, to whom any form of pageantry and tom-foolery was preferable to work.'

All this was music to many English ears, and disquieting even to those on whom it grated. If real support in Ireland for Home Rule was narrow or factional, or largely that of riff-raff, or from a few agitators, then for Britain to concede it would exhibit neither justice nor political acumen, but rather weakness and stupidity. Such mis-givings were accentuated by another aspect of the Unionist campaign. In order to spread their picture of what Home Rule would mean, Unionists sought to discredit the Ireland that wanted Home Rule by showing it — sometimes directly, with lantern slides — as the home of outrage and atrocity, degradation and barbarism: to get what they wanted, they denigrated their own country, confirming the already highly adverse images of Ireland that prevailed in Britain. Another salient feature in the Unionist depiction of Home Rule was the assertion that it would be Rome rule. Whatever the sincerity or otherwise of that belief, there can be no doubt that Unionists set out deliberately to arouse English and particularly Scots bigotry in their support.

All of this, as will be seen, fitted into dominant English presumptions. Supporters of Home Rule had constantly emphasized as contradictory the refusal to give Ireland Home Rule, and English support for European nationalist movements, especially the Italian. The only convenient escape from this accusation of inconsistency was the denial of the reality of Irish nationalism and its branding as a sham and a fraud. Long before the emergence of the Ulster question, English opinion had refused to concede the integrity of Irish nationalism. It was seen as totally destructive, without positive virtues, simply a gust of anti-English hate. 'What is the meaning of Irish nationality?' asked *The Times* in 1848. 'It seeks to destroy English institutions, abolish the English language, root out the common law, abolish trial by jury.' Or it was dismissed as mere congenital commotion — in a favoured English pun of the time, Pat-riot-ism. Particularly in its stronger expressions, such as Fenianism, it was characterized as mad and criminal, lacking even the semblance of the moral and political stature possessed by European nationalisms. These traditional attitudes had been declining in strength as the Home Rule movement grew in power and acceptability, but Ulster propaganda did much to revive them.

However, the harm done to the relationship lay also in the effect Ulster's words and actions had within Ireland. Nationalists reacted by asserting their position even more vigorously: from 1913 Ulster extremism in organization and acquisition of arms became one of the examples extreme nationalism in the south sought to follow. As for Unionists, they succeeded in persuading at least themselves that no real nationalist movement existed, or that it should be properly ignored or repressed, a conviction that has persisted until the present day. They constructed for themselves an image of Irish nationalism as being a destructive aberration proceeding from the minds of cunning priests and fanatical demagogues. Ernest Hamilton was even capable of putting it all down to Irish whiskey: '. . . any devil with a glib tongue and a gallon of potheen can sway the proletariat as he will. Potheen . . . emanates from secret stills in the mountains, and pays no duty, but its effect on human nature is bad — maddening and brutalizing — and taken in quantities, it quickly transforms kindly, peaceable men into fully-equipped fiends.'

At the centre of all this contention was the Union. By the mid-nineteenth century, the Union was carrying an enormous weight of responsibility for things well beyond its orbit, and this weight increased with the years. In both England and Ireland, matters of identity, survival, pride, and self-esteem were all caught up in the question of the survival or otherwise of the Union. Thomas Macaulay's representative English proposition, 'The repeal of the Union we regard as fatal to the Empire', became elevated into a matter of faith and emotion rather than being held as a reasoned conclusion. Crude strategic considerations were to remain important in English attitudes towards Ireland down to the Second World War, but by the 1880s these were accompanied by considerations of historical prestige and a kind of geographical mystique based on an image of British greatness. To the Irish nationalist assertion that geography had made Ireland, as an island, into a separate nation, the supporters of the United Kingdom replied, as did Asquith in 1912, with the claim that nature had made the British Isles a unit. A.V. Dicey in *England's Case Against Home Rule* (1886) added to this the argument of historical experience. He took the line that the British Isles was a geographic integrity over which the English crown had become ascendant, thus creating one British nation. To undo this natural and traditional union would be to go against the logical flow of history. It would be interpreted by the world as a sign of national decline, and would in fact be so. The greatness of Great Britain had a physical expression, and to diminish this at its very centre would be a self-destructive act, and a betrayal of those values that gave Britain its pre-eminence in civilization.

For Unionists within Ireland such arguments were made much more compelling by their belief that they would be the first casualties of this destructive process: their very survival demanded retention of the Union. Irish nationalists were no less convinced that their kind of Ireland depended for its future on the severance or at least modification of the Union. For them, the Union had come to be seen as the fount of all Irish evils: remove it and Ireland would be born again, this time truly itself. So, to all parties involved in the Union, their fate and future came to seem utterly dependent on what happened to the Union. This belief produced profound distortions, fostered the taking of extreme positions and impelled the adoption of extreme methods. It also had great staying-power as well, as may be judged from the continuance of the issue into contemporary times.

Seen thus, the matter of the Union was a matter of survival. But it would be false to interpret the issue as

confined to selfish interests and impulses, for its dimensions
were much wider, involving as it did values and convictions
seriously and sincerely held. There existed, among some
Englishmen, a real and painful sense of responsibility
towards Ireland, based on a genuine belief—bereft of
arrogance—that England's superior gifts imposed duties in
regard to Ireland: this is well-delineated, as a mood and a
set of impulses rather than any coherent philosophy, by
Elizabeth Bowen in her novel of the Anglo-Irish war, *The
Last September*.

Kipling, the poet of imperialism, expressed neatly the
English resolution of the conflict between the imperial
dream and reality:

> *'If England was what England seems*
> *An' not the England of our dreams,*
> *But only putty, brass, and paint*
> *'Ow quick we'd drop her! but she aint!'*

Some Irish were brought to share this dream — Protestant
Ulstermen certainly did—but to the majority, England was
what England seemed. That anyone should prefer a
debased Irish way of life to identification with the glory and
wealth of England seemed, to the majority of Englishmen,
quite absurd. Writing in 1949, Rebecca West could readily
understand why the father of William Joyce (Lord Haw
Haw) left Ireland in 1922, after it had become Eire. He was
one of those sensible Irishmen 'who honestly loved law and
order and preferred the smart uniforms and soldierly
bearing of the English garrisons and the Royal Irish
Constabulary to the furtive slouching of a peasantry
distracted by poverty and revolutionary fever.' However, a
few perceptive Englishmen did find intelligible the Irish
preference for their own life-style. Matthew Arnold was one
such: 'English civilization means to the Irish the civilization
of our middle class; and few indeed are the attractions
which to the Irish, with their quickness, sentiment, fine
manners and indisposition to be pleased with things
English, that civilization seems . . . to have . . . our
civilization has no courtesy and graciousness, it has no

enjoyment of life, it has the curse of hardness upon it . . .'

And Arnold concluded that 'the pedantry, bigotry, and narrowness of our middle class, which disfigure the civilization we have to offer, are also the chief obstacle to our offering measures perfectly healing'. In Arnold's view, as long as the middle class remained what it was, relations with Ireland could never be made satisfactory—and he foresaw little prospect of that class changing.

It remains now to attempt to explain in some detail how that class, and Englishmen generally, saw the Irish, and how they came to hold views so unfavourable, and so uncomprehending.

At least some of the inconsistencies and contradictions which marked English attitudes towards the Irish can be resolved into a dualism attached to the peasant image. This was, predominantly and realistically enough, the dominant English image of the Irish: as the Irish poet Brian Friel remarked recently, 'that is what we still are—a peasant people'. At least since Thomas Davis in the 1840s, Irish nationalism had recognized this not only as a fact, but as a desirable fact. Once liberated from landlordism and allowed the free development of its traditional culture, the peasantry would constitute the heart and soul—and the body—of the true Irish nation. However, as Brian Friel has pointed out in an Irish context, 'Peasant is an emotive word. It evokes sympathy (saint, dreamer, pure, individual, pastoral) or disgust (ignorant, vulgar, philistine, thick)'. Irish nationalism took the sympathetic view: the dichotomy remained in the English reaction, but with a strong leaning towards the unfavourable estimate.

This dichotomy had been reflected, and fostered within, the literary depiction of the Irish peasantry, at least since the first publication of William Carleton's enormously popular *Traits and Stories of the Irish Peasantry* in 1830. The preface to the 1854 edition shows Carleton himself to have been very conscious of the implications of his work for the formation outside Ireland of a view of Irish conditions and character. He acknowledged the existence of two extremes—the twisted savage terrorist. of 'Wildgoose

Lodge', and the fun-loving innocent gossoon of 'Phelim O'Toole's Courtship'. This happier image had a continued existence in England, its currency sustained particularly by the Anglo-Irish vision of Ireland expressed at its amusing best by Somerville and Ross in *Experiences of an Irish RM* (1899). In this picturesque image, the peasant, quaint, loveable and childlike, exists as a colourful and subordinate background to a world in which English or Anglo-Irish dominance, exercised as a kind of aristocratic benevolence, was stable and unquestioned. This was a view of Ireland especially intelligible and appealing to the English. It was certainly part of the truth — Somerville and Ross wrote from experience, and recorded observation — but it was also a depiction which suited the English view of what the Anglo-Irish relationship should be like — English or Anglo-Irish gentry ruling a placid and entertaining population of family retainers.

In periods of relative calm, this harmless, engaging image tended to blot out the spectre of the terrorist, at least among the literate and genteel, thus heightening the alarm and dismay when violence broke out again. This reaction is illustrated by Elizabeth Bowen in *The Last September* through the character of Mrs Vermont, wife of an English officer serving during the Irish 'Troubles':

'. . . Who would ever have thought of the Irish turning out so disloyal — I mean, of course, the lower classes! I remember mother saying in 1916 — you know when that dreadful rebellion broke out — she said: "This *has* been a shock to me; I never shall feel the same about the Irish again!" You see, she had brought us all up as kiddies to be so keen on the Irish and Irish songs . . . She always said they were the most humorous people in the world, and with hearts of gold. Though of course we had none of us ever been in Ireland.'

The fact was, that there were groups in Ireland whose existence supported a benign English image — those who behaved as the English thought they ought to; notably the Anglo-Irish, the 'Castle Catholics' (those middle-class Irish Catholics who supported the English administration) and

later, from the 1880s, to the First World War, the Ulster
Unionists. All these professed and evidenced loyalty, and
supported the kind of social values deemed appropriate to
their place in society. There was a strong English tendency
to see particularly the Anglo-Irish as *the* Irish, or at least
the only Irish who really mattered. After all, the Anglo-
Irish were the Irish establishment, their social links with the
English establishment were close and frequent, theirs were
the names that dominated the professions and public life,
and most of Irish art and letters, they were intimately and
prominently involved in the British imperial enterprise as
army officers and colonial administrators, and when they
spoke, their accents were English—they took care to
preserve themselves from the brogue. These Irish were
readily acceptable to the English of the same class, and
shared their values, holding in abhorrence 'bad form,
poverty, patriotism, activity, nationality, curiosity, and
Popery'—under all of which heads the native Irish were, to
use the appropriate contemptuous phrase, beyond the Pale,
unacceptable, of no real account.

The English tendency to assume that the Anglo-Irish
were of more account than the Celtic masses was reinforced
by another wishful assumption—that Irish Catholics would
be loyal and properly behaved if they were not the victims of
unscrupulous demagogues and priestcraft. This conviction
led to occasional crusades to redeem the Irish from their
ignorance and superstition, crusades directed towards
the spread of English values and education through
appropriate schools and religious teaching. The presumption was that these things, good in themselves,
would also wean the mass of the Irish from their subjection
to the few crafty and envenomed self-seekers, who had
imposed their perverted leadership on them. The British
army and the Royal Irish Constabulary appeared to offer
evidence which supported this proposition, though it might
be argued equally well that the very substantial Irish
element in the rank and file of the British army and navy
(somewhere about a third throughout the nineteenth
century) necessitated—in terms of retaining confidence in

forces so composed — the assumption that, under the authority and discipline of an English-officered situation, the Irish were transformed. Whether expedient or sincere, this belief in the transformatory power of English authority situations was prevalent in relation to the Irish: the interpretation is clearly set out in J.A. Froude's comment made during his 1841 tour of Ireland: 'The inhabitants, except where they had been taken in hand and meta-morphosed into police, seemed more like tribes of squalid apes than human beings.'

The English image of Ireland in its benign form, occupied so largely by the acceptable Anglo-Irish, and by misled, but ultimately reformable masses, was notable for its tendency to find what it wanted to see. Writing in 1881, Matthew Arnold regarded this as the major barrier to a solution of the Irish question: 'The true explanation of any matter is therefore seldom come at by us, but we rest in that account of things which suits our class, our party, our leaders, to adopt and to render current. We adopt a version of things because we choose, not because it really represents them; and we expect it to hold good because we wish that it may.'

In the case of Ireland '. . . the prejudices of our two most influential classes, the upper class and the middle class, tend always to make a compromise together, and to be tender to one another's weaknesses; and this is unfortunate for Ireland . . . Our aristocratic class does not firmly protest against the unfair treatment of Irish Catholicism, because it is nervous about the land. Our middle class does not firmly insist on breaking with the old evil system of Irish landlordism, because it is nervous about Popery'.

Such English prejudice and wishful thinking could survive as political determinants largely because of their existence remote from the realities of the emotional atmosphere in Ireland. Confronted with direct experience of Ireland, sensitive and perceptive English minds felt the hatred like a blow, and were appalled by England's ignorance of this situation. J.H. Newman wrote in 1866: 'How dark, as even I could see, we are as to Ireland, from having been there . . .' He marked 'the hatred felt for England in all ranks in Ireland . . . great friends of mine did not scruple to speak to me of the "bloody English"—the common phrase—. . . cautious and quiet government people simply confessed they would gladly show their teeth if they were sure of biting . . . Every Irishman is but watching his opportunity—and if he is friendly to this country it is because he despairs.' In 1881, the English visitor W.H. Duignan made almost identical observations and arrived at a similar conclusion. All this was simply not believed in England.

Newman was one of the very few Englishmen who understood why the Irish should feel and act as they did: 'If I were an Irishman, I should be (in heart) a rebel,' he wrote in 1887. Others exposed to the shock of that hatred did not understand it and were horrified and indignant, for they could see no real cause or justification for it. In some Irishmen, this hatred was simple and primitive, but for the literate educated class it was sometimes complicated by their indebtedness to English culture. W. B. Yeats explained: 'No people hate as we do in whom the past is always alive, there are moments when hatred poisons my life and I accuse myself of effeminacy because I have not given it adequate expression . . . [but] everything I love has come to me through English; my hatred tortures me with love, my love with hate.' Yeats was to immortalize the destructive effects of this hate as an element in Irish nationalism:

> We had fed the heart on fantasies,
> The heart's grown brutal from the fare;
> More substance in our enmities
> Than in our love . . .

That hatred, made holy, was a prominent feature of the nationalism of 1916. P.H. Pearse praised the Fenian O'Donovan Rossa in these terms: '. . . for the English he had a hatred that was tinctured with contempt. He looked upon them as an inferior race, morally and intellectually; he despised their civilization: he mocked at their institutions and made them look ridiculous.'

Some Irishmen maintained that this hatred was not directed towards the English as a people, or towards individual Englishmen. Casement claimed that his hatred for England was 'wholly impersonal, just as we are told to hate *Sin*'. Or as a man at Dungavan said to an English visitor in 1881, 'Ah! sir, we hate the government so much we have nothing but love left for Englishmen and all strangers'. Despite this reaction of automatic politeness, it is doubtful if many Irishmen made such a distinction. More likely is the truth of T.P. O'Connor's observation that 'To the Irishman who has never left the Irish shores, the Englishman, by a fallacious generalization, was embodied, not in his own personal character, but in the regime that was supposed to support and to represent him'.

Nevertheless, the Irish were subjected to the same tactical and emotional pressures as induced the English to make a distinction between leaders and people: to accept the existence of a monolithic English hostility to all Ireland's objectives was altogether too despairing. So, there existed in Ireland a strong presumption that the English people wanted to give justice to Ireland, but were being constantly frustrated by a tiny but powerful minority of Tory landowning elements in influential places. (A parallel Irish illusion was that the people of Ulster really wanted Home Rule, but were being misled by a few bigots.) This tendency to draw a sharp distinction between a supposedly benign English people and a malign English government was an important characteristic of the attitudes of those Irishmen — notably the Irish parliamentary party and its leading supporters — who sought constitutional reforms and concessions *via* the English political system. It was necessary for them to believe that the system was capable of and willing to produce Irish reform, and if parliament was resistant it must be because it did not represent as yet the true will of a sympathetic English people.

This attitude was a source of distortion and confusion within England as it presented an Irish face which seemed both co-operative and respectful, indeed deferential, as represented for example by John Redmond (taken in

England to be nationalist Ireland's leader and spokesman)
who showed his veneration and admiration for British
institutions and empire. Redmond was far from typical.
Michael Davitt's estimate of the English was much more
prevalent:

'They are a nation without faith, truth or conscience,
enveloped in a panoplied Pharisaism and an incurable
hypocrisy. Their normal appetite is fed on falsehood. They
profess Christianity and believe only in Mammon. They talk
of liberty while ruling India and Ireland against the
principles of a Constitution professed as a political faith but
prostituted to the interests of class and landlord rule.'

This kind of nationalist generalization was often
accompanied by an image of the English personal character
no less superficial and stereotyped — and adverse — than was
the English view of the Irish: 'All alike,' Canon Sheehan's
Luke Delmege concluded of Englishmen, 'Made out of
putty and then frozen.' It was a common Irish estimate that
the English were cold, hypocritical, arrogant, greedy and
above all, fools — unaware of what life was about and of
what was going on around them.

No less bewildering to the English was the countenance of
Ulster Protestantism. This could appear as ultra-British, or
as willing to fight Britain in order to remain British, or even
as pro-German. It was beyond English understanding that
while Ulster Protestants venerated English institutions, the
Empire, and the abstract idea of England, England in
practice, as it actually existed, its policies and people, were
not much to their taste. Ulstermen, seeing themselves
as both English and Irish, disliked — in their Irish in-
carnation — being subjected to English patronage, while
in their English aspect they came to believe that the English
were beginning to abandon in weakness the principles of
history and religion that made England truly England.
Ulstermen were no less image ridden about England than
were the nationalist Irish — and neither image was
acceptable to the English themselves. The Ulster assumption that the true England was that of the Protestant
constitution of 1688, from which any departure was a

betrayal and a sacrifice of vital principles, was not widely shared in England, and indeed it bred resentment in England that Ulster should presume to insist on its self-interested definition of what the constitution should be. English Unionists did not take up the cause of Ulster out of any warm feeling of commonality with its inhabitants. It simply suited their politics to do so. In 1886 Lord Randolph Churchill identified himself with Ulster's opposition to Home Rule out of simple expediency: he believed it would forward his own conservative political purposes within Britain. English Unionists had no particular care for Ireland but saw the Ulster situation as a tactically useful ground for fighting Home Rule which they opposed on imperial grounds. If Ulster Protestants had little love for an England they saw as supine, degenerate, and unreliable, the English temperament, particularly in its liberal form, reacted strongly against the salient features of the militant Ulster Protestants. 'An Irish Orangeman cannot argue, he is full of passion and prejudice, and having been so long under Protentant ascendancy, he cannot realize the principle of political equality. To make discussion agreeable, or even possible, I found it necessary always to yield or change the subject' — such was an English visitor's experience in 1884. The marked distaste which Englishmen felt for Ulster, its attitudes and atmosphere, is one of the factors which caused England to virtually ignore Ulster after 1921.

Generally, an England becoming increasingly industrial, urban, and wealthy, was out of sympathy with a poor peasant culture seen as inferior and unprogressive. But it was direct domestic experience in the early nineteenth century that did most to establish, at a most crucial stage in England's own history, a radically unfavourable image of the Irish.

The first decades of the nineteenth century saw a substantial Irish emigration to England, Wales, and Scotland: by 1841 over 400,000 Irish-born resided there, a figure which takes no account of descendants, or of the large number of temporary or seasonal migrants. This amounted to nearly 2 per cent of the population of England and Wales, and nearly 5 per cent of that of Scotland. By 1851, these percentages had risen to nearly 3, and over 7: in that year there were 727,326 Irish-born living in England, Wales, and Scotland. The image-making impact of this massive immigration was greatly heightened by its character and concentration, as well as by its inflation by the great numbers of migrants in transit to America.

Its character was that of extreme poverty, and it concentrated in the industrial cities and in the worst sections of those cities. The 1861 census showed the Irish-born to be most strongly concentrated in western Scotland and in the north-western counties of England: they were a quarter of the population of Liverpool. Add to this their descendants, and the fact that the Irish congregated in what amounted to ghettos,[3] and it is evident that the Irish presented an inescapable and highly disturbing feature of the new British urban industrial landscape.

The influx from Ireland coincided with the growth in the new industrial towns of problems of poverty, overcrowding, misery, and disease. This coincidence was taken as a simple cause-effect relationship, so that the Irish, their nature and habits, were held to be responsible for conditions of squalor and unrest. Certainly the areas in which the Irish lived exhibited the worst and most degraded aspects of urban industrialized England. But whereas the Irish were the victims of the evils of the Industrial Revolution, which they exhibited in a spectacular way, they were held to have brought them about. As the Glasgow *Commonwealth* remarked with some irony in 1854: 'To Ireland, it appears, we are indebted to this somewhat large mass of civic poverty, drinking, swearing, and sometimes fighting in our midst.' As if such evil inclinations were foreign to the innocent Scots and English, the vices and problems of the growing cities were attributed to the incursions of the Irish. It might well be argued that the Irish were made the

---

[3] The legitimacy of the term 'ghetto' as applied to the Irish situation in Britain has been questioned, but there seems every reason to accept it as appropriate to at least the first half of the nineteenth century. See John Werly, 'The Irish in Manchester', 1832–49' *Irish Historical Studies*, Vol. xvii, no 71, March 1973.

scapegoat for that great confusion of emotions, impulses, and prejudices generated by the development of the Industrial Revolution in Britain — pride, fear, guilt, shame, optimism, self-confidence, righteousness, indignation, belief in progress..

Extreme poverty, peculiar customs, and unruly behaviour were not, of course, confined to the Irish, but there was much in their circumstances, characteristics, and behaviour which made them distinctive, and the object of particular distaste and hostility. They lived apart, in ghettos marked by conditions so revolting that the better class of English workman would not live near them. Nor was there much social mixing. Even the kind of work the Irish did tended to segregate them. According to the 1836 report on the Irish poor, they had obtained exclusive possession of all the lowest departments of manual labour. This apartness was reinforced by the language situation. Most Irishmen could speak English, but A.M. Sullivan found, on a visit to the Black Country in 1856, that they spoke Irish at home, if only because their wives could speak no other language. When they spoke English it was with a brogue that emphasized their distinctiveness.

Then there was the matter of behaviour. The keeping of animals in houses was particularly repellent to English taste, but it was when he was out of his house that the Irishman gave most offence. First, there seemed so many of them. There were indeed a great number, but because many were vagrants or beggars, and because the Irish were prominent in the street trade and the servant class, they were frequently encountered and thus made an exaggerated public impression. Besides, on the streets, their behaviour was at best ebullient, and at worst, such as in the spectacular drunken brawls endemic to Saturday nights in Liverpool, Manchester and other cities, violent and even riotous. They attracted trouble, particularly sectarian riots, and absorbed a great deal of police attention. Their tendency to wild drunkenness was a by-word. So was their reputation for criminality, if only of a relatively minor sort. The outcome of all this was that respectable bourgeois

Britain formed a strongly unfavourable image of the Irish, regarding them, to take the words of the 1836 Report on the Irish Poor, as 'a less civilized population spreading themselves, as a kind of substratum, beneath a more civilized community . . .' Not only did they stridently exhibit their lack of civilization, they lacked the virtues most revered in Victorian England: they showed no thrift or forethought, accepted poor relief without shame, and were addicted to vulgar emotional display. One of the prominent criteria by which the English evaluated the Irish was that of the work ethos. When this was applied to the Irish in Ireland, the Irish appeared utterly contemptible. *The Times* asked in 1847, 'What is an Englishman made for but to work? What is an Irishman made for but to sit at his cabin door, read O'Connell's speeches, and abuse the English?' According to *The Times*, the besetting sin of Ireland was idleness — allied with reliance on the industry of others, namely the English. The outcome was a parasitic ingratitude: as Ian Hay expressed it in 1918, 'Ireland appropriates all her [England's] spare cash and calls her a blood sucker'.

The undoubted observable fact that the Irish who came to Britain demonstrated remarkable energy and capacity to cope with hard work did not cause English questioning of why they should be idle and lethargic in Ireland itself. An obvious possible explanation, one favoured by Irish reformers, was that English policy, particularly in regard to the Irish land system, destroyed all incentive and reduced Irish economic life to torpor. But the English conclusion was that the industry of the Irish when they came to Britain merely proved the superiority of the total English environment to that of Ireland: transplant the Irishman from that land of bogs, superstition, and political perversity, and he would soon reveal, under the benign influence of a true civilization, capacities previously unseen. Yet the fact that the Irish in Britain worked hard did not endear them to the British middle classes. They also played hard and drank hard, and showed no real wish to better themselves. Not only did they seem content to remain in the lowest tasks, but they refused to take work in that serious way, as if some exercise in piety, approved by bourgeois England. As to their fellow-workers, the Irish competition for jobs, and their willingness to accept lower wages or act as strike breakers, alienated them from working class Britain. Besides which, as Marx pointed out in 1870, the English worker 'feels himself a member of the ruling nation . . . He cherishes religious, social and national prejudices against the Irish worker'.

The image of the Irish as degraded and uncivilized bred a great deal of resentment among the Irish themselves. Both the intensity of this image and the resentment it came to engender may be explained, at least in part, by a line of argument put forward by Professor Emmet Larkin. He suggests that the pre-famine, and famine years of Irish emigration created a false, or rather a very partial image of the Irish within the countries to which they emigrated. The emigration of that time represented a society marked by poverty, ignorance, violence, drunkenness, and viciousness, one which was substantially irreligious: all of these repellent characteristics reached their depths during the famine. However, the famine swept that culture away, and the new Ireland that grew from the desolation was more prosperous, less crude, and certainly much more religious in its values. This Ireland was much more acceptable in terms of what England took to be the standards of civilization, but by this time the image derived from the earlier experience had been firmly set and was deeply resistant to change.

But there was more to British hostility than cultural revulsion. There was also suspicion and fear. This was composed of several elements. One was the matter of health. The crowded squalor of Irish settlements in major British cities bred disease, and the appearance of cholera and typhus, particularly in 1847-8, was a sharp stimulus to anti-Irish clamour. Then there was the matter of expense, particularly the burden the Irish placed on poor relief. The *Glasgow Herald* complained in 1853: 'We have thus to bear the expense of supporting the lives of perhaps the most improvident, intemperate and unreasonable beings that exist on the face of the earth, who infest us in shoals and beg our charity because the land of their birth either cannot or will not support them. Our hospitals are filled with them, our police are overwrought by them, our people are robbed and murdered by them.'

And then there was the question of danger to the security of the nation. Historically—and this was at the crux of the relationship—the English viewed the Irish as potential traitors. Confronted with serious unrest in Ireland, a first English assumption was that it was impelled by internal sedition if not foreign connections: experience seemed to support this interpretation particularly since implementation of the principle 'England's difficulty is Ireland's opportunity' tended to present England with Irish challenges which appeared to be part of some general threat, from continental powers, or from revolutionary ideologies. Even if such a linkage was not apparent, and Irish agitation could be seen to derive from particular and local causes, the English regarded it as creating a dangerous situation of a wider kind, in either inviting foreign intervention, or in allowing the submerged Irish forces of sedition to surface once again. A tough policy on all unrest was, therefore, expedient for security reasons, with the consequence that causes rooted, not in sedition, but in the socio-economic situation were disregarded. And to treat all unrest as sedition and disloyalty was to ensure that eventually it became so.

This frame of mind was carried over both to apply to and be sustained by, the activities and presence of the Irish in England. Suspicion and alarm felt in England fed on and nurtured suspicion and alarm concerned with Ireland, and vice versa. The 1798 Irish rebellion was seen as the expression of a wider movement of Catholic sedition and Jacobinism. From an early stage, the massive Irish concentration amongst the lower orders in England was taken as indicative of radical potential and socially disruptive intention. In 1848 it seemed that the Irish, the Chartists and those influenced by foreign revolutionary ideas were all part of the same menace. The businessmen of

Liverpool sought suspension of *habeas corpus* and enrolled 3,000 special constables to deal with the anticipated social revolution. Incendiarism in Kent and Surrey produced a crop of rumours that French and Irish agents, together with 'itinerant Radicals' were travelling around the country fomenting violence. In Kent, riots and fires were attributed variously to the work of smugglers, Papists, O'Connell's agents, the government, bigoted Protestants, radicals, and foreign revolutionaries. Whatever the vision of revolution, terrorism and anarchy in vogue, Irish Catholics were always central to it. The Irish bogey in England was given some substance by the hopes and intentions of Irish revolutionaries. At one of his meetings in Liverpool in 1848 Terence Bellew McManus announced the intention of placing England in a state of seige: it was proposed to further the chances of revolution in Ireland by keeping as many troops as possible engaged in confrontations in England and Scotland.

In fact, with a few exceptions, such as Bronterre O'Brien, and Feargus O'Connor, the Irish in Britain took little part in agitation for social reform and did not identify themselves significantly with working class movements.[4] The attitude of the Irish in Britain towards the society in which they worked tended to be passive acceptance, not hostility or aggression. It provided them with a living they could not get in Ireland, and they were no less than tolerant towards a goose whose eggs, if not golden, were acceptable enough to prompt little complaint. There was more substance in English fears of unrest springing from specifically Irish political causes and grievances. The triumphal tours of, for example, O'Connell and Parnell, of Irish centres in Britain were regarded with some trepidation and certainly with disfavour. Until the 1860s, such activities

[4] The conclusion of John Hickey (*Urban Catholics. Urban Catholicism in England and Wales from 1829 to the present day* (London, 1967) pp. 135–44) seems to conflict with E. P. Thompson's view *(The Making of the English Working Class* (London, 1963) pp. 441–3) that there was a clear alliance between Irish nationalism and English radicalism between 1790 and 1850. The important matter for present purposes is not the question of the extent of this alliance, but rather the extent of contemporary belief in its existence.

produced little more than money to support Irish causes, but the emergence of Fenianism came to pose a more concrete threat within Britain itself, a threat which was eventually to issue in a wave of hysteria in the late 1860s. The threat that Britain might be infected by the contagion of Irish violence, or at least have its own domestic affairs complicated by matters Irish, did not abate. By 1885 not only had the Home Rule movement been embraced enthusiastically by the Irish in Britain, but their vote had become sufficiently effective to return the nationalist T.P. O'Connor in Liverpool. Five years later the Irish National League was a force in British politics not only at the parliamentary, but at the municipal level. In reality, the Irish were not—with the occasional exception—an enemy in the English midst, but from time to time they appeared so.

Just how intense was the fear and how deep the antagonism and prejudice is clearly illustrated in Thomas Carlyle's observations on the Irish in 1839, significantly in relation to the theme of Chartism.

'Crowds of miserable Irish darken all our towns. The wild Milesian features, looking false ingenuity, restlessness, unreason, misery and mockery, salute you on all highways and byways . . . He is the sorest evil this country has to strive with. In his rags and laughing savagery, he is there to undertake all work that can be done by mere strength of hand and back; for wages that will purchase him potatoes. He needs only salt for condiment; he lodges to his mind in any pighutch or doghutch, roosts in outhouses . . . The Saxon man if he cannot work on these terms finds no work. He too may be ignorant; but he has not sunk from decent manhood to squalid apehood.'[5]

Using the Irish to represent the ultimate in degradation, Carlyle, like other English observers, built up a contrasting image of the English character which exalted just those

---

[5] Later direct experience was to confirm Carlyle's judgement of the Irish. See Thomas Carlyle, *Reminiscences of My Irish Journey in 1849* (London, 1882). A visit to the Westport workhouse convinced him that 'Human swinery has here reached its *acme* . . .' (p. 201).

virtues and qualities the Irish were supposed not to possess:
'. . . that the Saxon British will ever submit to sink along
with them [the Irish] to such a state, we assume as impossible'. He saw in the Saxon 'an ingenuity which is not
false; a methodic spirit, of insight, of perseverant well-
doing; a rationality and veracity . . . justice, clearness,
silence, perseverance, unhasting unresting diligence, hatred
of disorder, hatred of injustice, which is the worst disorder,
characterize this people'.

Yet — strange example of the dualism at the heart of so
many English evaluations of Ireland — Carlyle cites English
injustice and violence as responsible for Ireland's woeful
condition: 'England is guilty towards Ireland; and reaps at
last, in full measure, the fruit of fifteen generations of
wrong-doing'. Carlyle appears both to have held that the
Irish were irredeemable, and that it was imperative that
they be redeemed. So: '. . . the oppression has gone far
farther than into the economics of Ireland; inwards to her
very heart and soul. The Irish National character is
degraded, disordered; till this recover itself, nothing is yet
recovered. Immethodic, headlong, violent, mendacious:
what can you make of the wretched Irishman? . . . A
people that knows not to speak the truth, and to act the
truth, such people has departed from even the possibility of
well-being. Such people works no longer on Nature and
Reality; works now on Phantom, Simulation, Non-
entity . . . Such a people circulate not order but disorder, through every vein of it; — and the cure, if it is to be a
cure, must begin at the heart: not in his condition only but
in himself must the Patient be all changed'. Yet: 'The time
has come when the Irish population must either be improved a little, or else exterminated . . .'

Why this urgent necessity, as discerned in 1839? Despite
his claim that the Saxon was proof against contamination,
Carlyle feared the baneful effects of English contact with
the Irishman, whom he saw 'as the ready-made nucleus of
degradation and disorder . . . the wretchedness of Ireland,
slowly but inevitably, has crept over us, and become our
own wretchedness. The Irish population must get itself

redressed and saved, for the sake of the English if for nothing else . . .' Others shared this fear. In a report on the sanitary state of Edinburgh in 1847, Dr Stark dated not only the physical but the moral deterioration of the lower classes from 1818, the year when began the influx of 'low Irish', building and canal labourers, who were 'the original and immediate cause of the deterioration of the lower classes'. Still others, whose concerns were religious and political rather than social and moral, feared that 'the wretched fecundity of Popish Ireland' would lead to its 'spreading ignorance and superstition over the empire' and would erode 'the integrity of all our national institutions'.

The fear and detestation of Popery was one of the foundations on which rested English — and Scots and Welsh — prejudice against the Irish. In 1851, in his *Lectures on the Present Condition of Catholics in England*, J.H. Newman went to the crux of that problem as a source of antagonistic imagery. Newman asked:

'. . . why it is, in this intelligent nation, and in this rational nineteenth century, we Catholics are so despised and hated by our own countrymen, with whom we have lived all our lives, that they are prompt to believe any story, however extravagant that is told to our disadvantage; as if beyond a doubt we were, every one of us, either brutishly deluded or preternaturally hypocritical, and they themselves, on the contrary were in comparison of us absolute specimens of sagacity, wisdom, uprightness, manly virtue, and enlightened Christianity . . . the Catholic Church is considered too absurd to be inquired into, and too corrupt to be defended, and too dangerous to be treated with equity and fair dealing. She is the victim of a prejudice which perpetuates itself, and gives birth to what it feeds upon.'

Newman discerned in the English an almost instinctive hostile reaction to all things Catholic stemming from the equation of Catholicism with both spiritual and political absolutism, and the belief that the Pope remained a dangerous political enemy of England, ambitious to possess her. Newman, as a convert from Anglicanism, was an excellent witness to the power of such images: even as Cardinal he confessed himself still beset by a 'stain on his imagination', the legacy of his upbringing, in his view of his own church. That images such as Newman described should be popular—that is, prevalent among ordinary people—was serious enough, but in fact adverse images of Catholicism were held in some degree by the leading statesmen, politicians, and public figures of England, virtually without exception.

The imagery of which Newman complained had much of its derivation from encounters with Catholic Ireland. It was injected with particular vigour by the coincidence of the Catholic revival in England—emancipation, the Oxford Movement, spectacular conversions and the restoration of the hierarchy—with efforts to meet Irish Catholic grievances (notably Peel's Maynooth Bill) and with a great influx of Irish Catholic immigrants. To the hostile British eye, every aspect of Catholic activity was linked, ominously and degradingly, with every other aspect. So, the condition of Ireland and the Irish proved the inferiority and depravity of their religion, whose nature was, of course, the main reason for that debased condition. And all of this was a direct threat not only to British religion, but to British prosperity, because 'The Reformed religion . . . is a developing principle, intellectual and industrial, and operates with beneficial effect on the worldly circumstances of its professors'.

Here then, is something of the world of images through which the history of Anglo-Irish relations moved. Some of it has endured. A Gallup Poll of August 1973 revealed that, despite years of booming economic progress in the south of Ireland, a quarter of Englishmen still regard it as poor. Nor do more than 5 per cent of Englishmen regard the southern Irish as intelligent or efficient. And it is hardly surprising that the English continue to appraise themselves as having the largest number of good attributes and the fewest bad ones. But images can be changed. Whereas in April 1968, only 8 per cent of Englishmen thought the Northern Irish to be intolerant, by August 1973, 44 per cent had reached that conclusion. The effect of that radically changed image on politics remains as yet to be revealed.

4

Politicians and Power

IT has been remarked by Nicholas Mansergh that England's inability to achieve a happy relationship with Ireland 'was not a failure for which this or that statesman could be held responsible, but it was a failure in the political conception of a nation'. But it would be absurd to exonerate statesmen entirely from responsibility: who more than politicians can be held to blame for prevalent political conceptions?

They were—perhaps to a large extent—inhibited by, if not prisoners of public opinion in England, as well as by needing to consider the wishes and interests of the ascendancy in Ireland. Even if politicians and newspaper editors might see an Irish measure as necessary or just, popular opinion or powerful vested interests seldom saw it that way. Perhaps politicians could also be described as the victims of their preconception that the sanctity of property was the bedrock of civilization, and that no interference with the rights of property was possible. On this rock foundered all efforts up the 1860s to reform the Irish land system. This conviction reflected social and legal conceptions derived from and applicable to the English situation, but exhibited total incomprehension of the different Irish scene. It was only in the 1860s that English politicians began to admit reluctantly the fact that, far from accepting English titles to land, the Irish peasantry rejected them in favour of their own historical claims prior to ancient dispossessions. Hitherto, where this had been noticed, it had been dismissed as a quaint and irrelevant relic. But in 1869, Sir Stafford Northcote, a liberal Tory, expressed a growing recognition that '. . . the national idea [in Ireland] of the relations of landlord and tenant is something totally different from the national idea in England . . . Undoubtedly the idea, whether right or wrong, of the Irish peasant is, that as long as he pays his rent and complies with the other conditions of what he considers his tenancy, he ought not to be evicted by his landlord. It is not a question whether that is so good as the mercantile idea, but whether it is one so rooted in the Irish mind that it is impossible to remove . . . If that be the case, you must provide for it accordingly'.

However, this realism was of narrow political extent. Many politicians were not prepared to provide for what they regarded as an Irish absurdity, nor would they concede any diminution of the mercantile idea, which, expressed in the primacy of legal contract, was the mark of progressive economic structure, whatever the primitive tenacity of the customs of a backward country.

It might also be reasonable to regard politicians as being trapped by the system through which they governed; as Goethe said, 'Their Parliamentary parties are great opposing forces which paralyse one another, and where the superior insight of an individual can hardly break through'. Perhaps this comment could be applied to Gladstone's situation, his efforts frustrated and cut back in parliament, when they might have solved the problem. Against this particular case, however, can be urged the argument that Gladstone's image as Ireland's champion takes insufficient account of his basic conservatism and orthodoxy: with his contemporaries, he accepted that the British Empire had a providential mission, and his Irish policy was directed towards maintaining the Empire, not weakening it.

Undoubtedly, in dealing with Irish problems, English politicians were beset by externally imposed limitations, but it is also difficult to avoid seeing them as imprisoned also by their own prejudices and inertia. The pattern is too clearly that of personal resistance or lack of interest: as Nassau Senior said of an ameliatory measure in 1843, 'as is too often the case in Irish matters it has been talked about, admitted to be useful, and dropped'. Reforms for Ireland were worth very few votes in England and prompted no apparent gratitude in Ireland. Indeed involvement in Irish affairs had a decided tendency to effect the destruction of personal careers and of ministries: some eleven nineteenth-century ministries became casualties of their Irish policies. To a large extent this may be traced to the division of opinion in English politics over how to respond to demands for change, whether to conciliate or coerce. This was a general clash of outlook, but Ireland happened to be the issue which raised questions of change most frequently, and in the most extreme or profound ways. The conflict between conciliators and coercionists was particularly damaging to Irish policies, which it tended to either paralyse, as neither programme could make way against the other in parliament, or delay and diminish beyond the point when reform policies could have been effective.

Naturally, the knowledge that this situation existed, acted as a deterrent to political initiatives, in relation to Irish issues. But any presumption that Ireland attracted the continued and serious attention of able English politicians intent on getting to the heart of the problem requires questioning. Some of the most prominent English politicians cared nothing for Ireland: both Disraeli and Lord Salisbury had no interest in Ireland, had never been there, and mixed ignorance and antipathy in fairly equal proportions. Robert Blake, Disraeli's biographer, has remarked that, in regard to the Irish, he 'never did or said anything helpful to them'. At some crucial times little or no trouble was taken to ascertain Irish facts. Because so few politicians had ever been to Ireland, those who had — particularly former Chief Secretaries — were particularly influential: their prejudices and personal opinions were accepted as objective fact. There are numerous cases of such reliance being baneful, particularly when such Chief Secretaries (Castlereagh and Wellesley Pole for instance) had strong Anglo-Irish family connections. Even Peel believed at the onset of famine in 1845 that a haze of exaggeration covered Dublin Castle like a fog: the distance factor led English politicians to exaggerate any cause for optimism and to discount bad news in the same way.

Then there is the matter of the calibre of English politicians. They afford ample illustration of blatant stupidity in regard to their comments on Irish matters. In 1868 Robert Lowe, Chancellor of the Exchequer, insisted that Fenianism should be left out of sight in discussing the Irish question because it had no connection with the land or church disestablishment issues. The extent among politicians of sheer mediocrity, cowardice, incompetence, and narrow party thinking is insufficiently appreciated. Hugh Holmes wrote of his Conservative cabinet colleagues in 1885:

'. . . I was surprised that so many occupants of the treasury bench were essentially commonplace and far below the intellectual standard required for success in literature and the learned professions. Two things however astonished me still more — first the timidity and want of moral courage which characterized the best of them, and secondly the thoughtless and haphazard way in which important resolutions were arrived at and carried out.

Lord Randolph Churchill was the only really courageous member of Lord Salisbury's first administration . . . But on the other hand he was especially casual and reckless in his political action . . . which was guided purely by party consideration, but in this respect he did not differ from his contemporaries.'

The consequences of Churchill's 'especially casual and reckless' political action in Ulster are still in train. In addition to that particular case, the general matter of the low intellectual quality, incompetence, and irresponsibility of English politicians is of considerable importance. It is part of the explanation of why Ireland was so neglected and misgoverned, and it illuminates that situation in which the reformist perceptions of intellectuals — such as Burke, Arnold, and Mill — so seldom had any issue in practical politics.

There was even serious failure in basic communications arising from differing understandings in Dublin and London of the meaning of terms. In 1846, the failure of the Westminster government to appreciate that in Ireland the

word 'farmer' referred to subsistence plot holders led to the
withholding of relief measures from men who were destitute
paupers, quite other than 'farmers' in the English context.
In 1867 Isaac Butt complained of precisely the same thing,
and again in relation to the land situation: 'Our misfortune
is that English phrases are applied to relations that bear no
resemblance to the things the words describe in the English
tongue'. In various ways, major and minor, terminology
was an important divisive force. Such words as 'secular' and
'non-sectarian' held commendatory or neutral connotations
in English political circles: used in Ireland they roused the
Irish episcopacy, particularly in regard to educational
matters, to fury and anathemas. The English use of such
words as 'loyalty' and 'law and order' because they were
judgement-laden, and served narrow and polemical
purposes, could arouse intense Irish hostility and
contempt.[1] The kind of alienation caused by an often
unconscious use of offensive phraseology was often
accompanied by apparent incomprehension of the value-
systems and traditional sensitivities of the Irish. In these
matters it was simply that the majority of Englishmen did
not appreciate that they were speaking or acting in a
context very different from their own.

Those English politicians who knew nothing or did
nothing about Ireland were important in their negative
ways in determining the course of Anglo-Irish relations. But
what of those who did act, and their motivation, and the
nature and results of the action they took? The period from
the 1870s to the First World War is the one in which Irish
affairs were continually at the forefront of British politics,
and thus the time during which the nature of British
political attention to Ireland is best examined.

What prompted that attention? Not any impulse from

---

[1] The English application of the description 'Sinn Fein' to the 1916 rebellion is
discussed by Joseph Sweeney 'Why "Sinn Fein"?', *Eire-Ireland*, vol. vi, no. 2,
Summer 1971, p. 39. England's policy in Ireland immediately before, during and
after the 1916 rebellion raises numerous questions in regard to the competence,
understanding and prudence of English politicians, administrators, and soldiers.
See Leon Ó Broin, *Dublin Castle and the 1916 Rising* (Dublin. 1966); Leon Ó
Broin, *The Chief Secretary, Augustine Birrell in Ireland* (London, 1969).

England, but the growing demand for Home Rule, particularly when backed by the aggressive tactics of Parnell. From 1877, Parnell's party, with its policies of parliamentary obstruction and disruption, and backed by the threat of peasant revolution, determined to rouse England and its politicians from complacency. It succeeded, but in a way which confirmed, among Liberals as well as Conservatives, the Irish image as one of turbulence and unscrupulousness. The intensity of the deep parliamentary revulsion occasioned by the Parnellite barbarian invasion may be gauged best not from Conservative tirades, but from the argument Gladstone's friend Lord Granville put forward in favour of Home Rule: it would remove the unruly and subversive Irish MPs, 'the dry rot in the . . . commons', from parliament, and, Granville maintained, the fact that it would get rid of this repulsive and dangerous element would make Home Rule palatable to a large majority. While it is true that Parnell's English origins and gentlemanly bearing were factors in commanding respect for his cause, to the English the prospect of getting rid of his band of Irish yahoos was no doubt an enticing one. But to many members, Home Rule appeared too high a price to pay for this boon. It would merely set up these uncivilized persons elsewhere, as a government, without restriction. To some Englishmen the matter of Home Rule was quite straightforward. Hugh Holmes held in 1886 that 'The single argument against it was that it handed over Ireland to the absolute control of a governing body bitterly hostile to Great Britain and that the power conferred by it would be used to destroy every link in the British connection. The more perfect the measure, the greater the danger . . .' The Gladstonian position was not to deny this danger but to contend that the danger was so real, that Home Rule, radical measure though that be, was the only means of avoiding it. Even those Englishmen who accepted Ireland's need for Home Rule often had great difficulty in reconciling this with their estimate of what this would mean for England. Cardinal Newman believed that the Irish should have Home Rule, 'But I am no advocate for such an issue, rather it seems to me a blow on the power of England as serious as it is retributive'. Common to the standpoints of those Englishmen who were for, against, or undecided about Home Rule was the belief that in one way or another the issue was associated with danger to English power: if some contended that it would avoid it, others were certain it would cause it. This was not an English atmosphere conducive to calm and generous deliberation.

Added to this, the emergence of the Home Rule issue in English politics in the 1870s coincided with a number of factors which combined to blacken its image. The Irish in the industrial areas of Britain had become, at least in theory, eligible for the vote in 1867, the year of the Fenian scare. The 1867 Reform Act filled Conservatives with foreboding: the social order would be invaded by a turbulent proletariat in which the Irish were a distinctive element, now even more to be feared as Fenians. This fear was given further substance by the existence of hope, among militant radicals, that the 1867 Act would be merely a first step towards the destruction of the power of the ruling landed classes. Certainly the development of the Home Rule movement in the 1870s was accompanied by a marked development in the political strength and organization of the Irish in Britain, a development in which ex-Fenians were prominent.[2] Indeed, Home Rule platforms in Britain in the 1870s were dominated by extreme Parnellites and ex-Fenians to a degree not obtaining in Ireland until the 1880s: Home Rule presented within Britain its most aggressive, intransigent face. This face was made uglier still, to the English, by the common practice among Home Rule campaigners of making arrogant threats, particularly that the Irish vote in Britain would be used, in seats where it was substantial, to coerce English parties into acceding to Irish demands. Both sides of the Home Rule issue greatly exaggerated the number of Irish voters, its champions in order to assert their potential power, its opponents to induce a sense of menace. In fact, the migratory and poor

[2] For this theme and period, I am indebted to Gearóid Ó Tuathaigh's unpublished paper, 'The Emergence of Home Rule in British Politics 1874-80'.

nature of the Irish population greatly decreased their voting potential, when qualification was usually related to a stable residence of over two years. It has been estimated, in a Glasgow context, that the actual political effectiveness of the Irish was perhaps half that suggested by their actual numbers: John Denvir claimed that in the mid 1880s, only about one in ten of the Irish population of Britain had the vote. However, such realities did not impinge on the alarm of those Englishmen who believed that the 1867 Act was a potentially grave blow to English political stability: here were the Irish promising to disrupt all English political life with their fanatical demand for Home Rule pursued by exploitation of the balance of power in English electorates and in parliament itself.

Other aspects of the Home Rule movement seemed no less disturbing. It appeared to be associated with the growing wave of land agitation and disorder which gathered in Ireland in the 1870s: the association became quite explicit with the New Departure of 1879. The Irish Land League, aside from its central position in sustaining resistance to English law and order, had a programme which rejected basic and orthodox English concepts of property rights and rent payment. Then there was the appalling behaviour of the Home Rule party in parliament, that of uncouth and unscrupulous ruffians, determined to disrupt the very institution by which the Empire was governed.

The idea that England might ever be at the mercy of the Irish prompted rage and fear, evident as early as 1877. To quote the *Salford Chronicle*: 'Shall the Home Rulers, a body of men utterly bankrupt in political intelligence, and totally devoid of political morality, dictate to English constituencies, and practically control the destinies of our vast Empire? . . . it is from the scum of our large towns that their ranks are recruited; ignorant, violent, turbulent; ready to be led by the nose by any brazen loud-tongued charlatan who chooses to bellow cheap sedition and frothy abuse of everything English; these men, forsooth, are the people who are to hold the balance between political parties in England, and decide the representation of English boroughs!'

By 1880, the image of Home Rule most widely accepted in England was that of disruption of English political life, eventual dismemberment of the Empire, and the handing-over of Ireland to anti-English terrorists, Romish priests, and masses of uncivilized land-thieving peasants. One does not need to resort to the statements of ultra-Tories to illustrate this image. In 1886, W. E. H. Lecky asserted in *The Times* that the impetus behind the Home Rule party was a communist desire to plunder the landlords, and an inveterate hatred of England. Nor would it be proper to neglect the standpoint of those impelled by conscience, not fear or self-interest, those who believed that Home Rule contradicted their basic conviction that politics ought to promote a better moral life. The Nonconformist radical W.S. Caine declared in 1886 that Home Rule was tantamount to capitulation to the Fenian 'outrage-mongers and boycotters' and would abandon the Irish to a Parnell-dominated regime of terrorism: this would negate the moral basis of politics, without any assurance that social improvement would ensue. Home Rule amounted to the abrogation of parliament's ethical and social responsibilities towards Ireland. Caine readily admitted the problem: it was simply that he regarded Home Rule as a cure worse than the disease, and that on firm moral grounds.

In such circumstances of English opinion, the wonder is that Home Rule made as much progress as it did. Up to 1885, that progress may be attributed to Parnell's effective tactics, and to the simple fact that an organized and determined Irish party was of sufficient size to compel attention. Thereafter, the cause of Home Rule became linked with the affairs of Gladstone and the Liberal Party.

The genuineness of Gladstone's adoption of Home Rule as a righteous principle need not be questioned in order to appreciate also its shrewdly calculated political motivation: the opposition of the Conservative party to Home Rule falls even more evidently into the category of selfish political manoeuvre, whatever elements of sincere conviction were also present. Recent research into the internal affairs of the Liberals and the Conservatives suggests that, in the 1880s, the Irish question came to be seen less as a scourge and more of a political godsend by both English parties.

Professor Hamer has surveyed some of the ways in which the English political preoccupation with Irish affairs can be interpreted as expressing the concerns and serving the needs of purely English politics. Was attention to Ireland a safety valve for feelings and attitudes generated within English politics by domestic concerns, such as fear of democracy or socialism, or of change generally? Was Ireland a means by which these concerns could be raised, debated and decided at a remove sufficiently far as to avoid fundamental and disruptive clashes on English ground? This is a subtle and elusive psychological area, but there is a good deal to support the more tangible proposition that Ireland was England's political laboratory a testing ground for, as well as a stimulus to, new policies.[3] Nor is it improbable that English political parties entered the Irish dimension of their world with motives and concerns substantially or even wholly English: it was natural that English politicians should put English politics first.

In considering such priorities in their historical context, a first question might be — were Irish matters regarded or employed as useful distractions from English issues that some people in England did not want pursued? Precisely this claim was made by John Morley in 1891: 'the man who hates change in England, the man who distrusts the look of present things and dreads the future, the man whose great object is to stem the democratic tide and to save his cherished inequalities and privileges, delights with his whole heart in keeping as long as he can, and for ever if he can, the two great political hosts of this country eternally clashing in the Irish ditch'.

Morley's charge could be dismissed as polemic, the attributing to the opponents of a Liberal solution to the Irish question of self-interested cunning rather than

---

[3] This orthodox view has been questioned by Joseph Lee, *The Modernization of Irish Society 1848-1918* (Dublin, 1973), pp. 34-5.

genuine objection. The depiction of England wrangling over Irish affairs to the neglect and retardation of English social reform, goes against the Marxist view that the Irish involvement was a radical modernizing force within British politics. However it is an interpretation given strong backing by Hamer's analysis of what was happening within the Liberal party.

By 1885 the morale and cohesion of the once triumphant Liberal party had declined into factionalism, incoherence, and even a weary wish to relinquish office. Such were the party's circumstances and mood that it is even possible to interpret its embracing of the Irish question as a form of political death-wish, or the courting of martyrdom. In the more positive view, Gladstone—for all his passion for Ireland as a noble cause—also saw it as a potential means of uniting and reviving the Liberal party: when his party split over Home Rule in 1886, he appears to have regarded this as a healthy purge of dissidents and the birth of a new phase of party unity. In 1888 Campbell-Bannerman made this explicit by thanking the Irish nationalists 'for having invented an Ireland and an Irish question, which had been a source of so much good and so much strength to the Liberal party'.

Liberals also claimed that Ireland absorbed so much time and political attention that quite insufficient remained for domestic reforms. They concluded that in order for these necessary English reforms to proceed, the Irish must be allowed, by Home Rule, to attend to their own affairs. Whatever the merits of this logic, it enabled Liberals to shelter behind Home Rule, so disguising their faults and avoiding distasteful or difficult tasks, notably that of devising a new domestic policy in rapidly changing times. Again, this situation was made explicit, in Lord Ripon's recommendation that the Liberal party retain Home Rule as its great policy because 'if it were displaced a whole series of labour questions would come to the front'—which was precisely the tactic which some in the labour movement believed the Liberals to be pursuing. This tactic was vitiated by the defeat of the second Home Rule Bill by the House of

Lords in 1894: the Lords and not Ireland was revealed to be the real obstacle to reform. But by this time the Liberals were irrevocably committed to Home Rule. What had been at least in part a tactic had become a commitment. By 1906 some Liberals saw it as a nuisance or a political liability, in that it diverted the party from the social programme desired by the electorate, and impaired party unity.

There is little doubt that however genuine was the Liberal championing of Home Rule, it was also seen by party leaders in narrow party terms as being a convenient and useful cause — and of course expedient, perhaps necessary for the health of England and the Empire. The question of which was the paramount consideration might find different answers for different times and different Liberals, but any picture of the Liberals' Irish policy as being the product of unanimous and undiluted altruism is demonstrably false.

Still more warranted are serious misgivings about the purity of Tory adoption of Unionism as a central principle. In the early 1880s, the Conservative party was deficient in ideas and policy, making do with a residuum of imperialism left over from Disraeli, and with a general hostility to all change. Having no real Irish policy, the party was looking for one, exhibiting in this an amalgam of confusion, negative attitudes and overall incompetence that astonished even those involved in the search. So far from a prior Tory commitment of principle to Unionism, it is possible that had the 1885 negotiations between Salisbury and Parnell reached a satisfactory conclusion, there might have issued a Tory initiative to concede Ireland some measure of self-government. This did not occur, and was, perhaps, unlikely, but it was a sufficient possibility to be matter for negotiations — which foundered less on a matter of Unionist principle than on the political likelihood that concessions to Ireland would split the Tory party. Political considerations were foremost in Lord Randolph Churchill's playing of the Orange card against Gladstone's Home Rule hand in 1886. He did so in order to test a possible winning policy, forward the interests of the Conservative cause and party in Britain and protect what he saw as the interests and honour of the Empire: the interests of Ireland seem hardly to have entered his mind. Ulster and the emotions and prejudices it might arouse were of political use to him and he exploited them without scruple, without responsibility, and without fear of the consequences. Churchill's arrogant unawareness of the danger of creating an Ulster Frankenstein — as well as his contemptuous disregard for Ulster — are evident in Lord Crewe's report of a conversation he had with him in 1893: 'I told him that the Unionists were making a great mistake in getting so closely tied up with Ulster, and they would pay for it when they wished to settle the question. Randolph replied "We shall tell Ulster to go to the devil," and I said, "That is exactly what you will never be able to do." '

Between 1886 and 1914, the essence of Conservative policy was Unionism as the nexus of imperial power and of the imperial ethos: the support of the crusade against Home Rule was central to this, with Ulster as focus, symbol and occasion. As has been pointed out by Professor Mansergh, Churchill's 'appeal for readiness and, if need be, resistance, was directed to Ulster, but it was not for Ulster. It was for the integrity of the empire that Ulster was to fight'. This needs to be borne in mind to appreciate how the policies of Conservative governments appeared to Irish nationalists. By 1895, Tory thinking on Ireland had settled firmly on the idea that preservation of the Union would be furthered best by Irish reforms, by 'killing Home Rule with kindness' as the cliché had it. The phrase made clear the motivation. The 'kindness' was not disinterested, a genuine effort to cope with Irish problems for Irish reasons: it had the explicit purpose of buying off Irish unrest and destroying the Home Rule movement. As such this policy was pilloried in Ireland, and as such what it gave earned no gratitude: it was seen for what it was — Irish legislation with an ultimately English and imperial purpose — and thus it had no long-term soothing effect on the relationship. No doubt it could be interpreted in a better light: in *Bowen's Court*, Elizabeth Bowen summarized Conservative policy as 'an attempt on the part of English gentlemen to treat the Irish as English gentlemen'. But she continued, 'Ironically, it was viewed on the Irish side of the water as either bribery or an admission of guilt'.

The close linkage which developed between the Conservatives and Ulster Unionists, in the mutual pursuit of narrow political advantage, was a vital factor in the active worsening of Anglo-Irish relations. This may be supported by an examination of the fate of Irish issues within English politics from 1906.

The 1906 election indicated that the normally low level of electoral reaction to Irish issues had dropped to virtually zero. The Liberals returned to power with a majority so large as to relieve them of dependence on Irish members. The electorate had moved decisively towards the Liberals despite their Irish policy, and away from the Unionists despite theirs: 'the Unionist leaders made a disastrous error of judgement . . . in believing that anti-radical opinion could·be rallied in 1906 over the cry of the union in danger' — so concludes Dr A.K. Russell's analysis of the election. Ireland had vanished as an issue, and the electorate's refusal to be scared by the Unionist depiction of Home Rule, or by the Liberals' commitment to that policy, indicated an atmosphere conducive to some Irish settlement.

The direct cause of the failure to take this opportunity was the self-interest of the Conservative party. At the constitutional conference of 1910, called to consider the issues raised by the Liberals' intention of depriving the House of Lords of its veto, Arthur Balfour made explicit the party's refusal to compromise on the matter of the Union. His major reason was party political: he believed that to drop intransigent Unionism would split his party, deprive it of its best fighting platform, and thus destroy its electoral chances for the indefinite future. The Unionist defeat in the 1910 elections, the third in succession and productive of the most intense bitterness and frustration, far from prompting any revision of this intransigence, confirmed it to the degree of obsession. Thereafter, their Irish policy, and exploitation

of the situation in Ireland, seemed to Unionists the only way
they might regain power. They therefore set about
exploiting it, with a degree of recklessness and
irresponsibility similar to that with which Randolph
Churchill had acquired the policy. Given its dependence on
its Irish policy, it was natural that the Unionist party should
come very much under the influence of Irish Unionists,
reflecting not merely their will, but their desperate resolve.
From 1910 'the Irish question dominated politics, squeezed
out progressive measures and attitudes, and brought the
United Kingdom to the verge of civil war'.

Such a situation developed because the English parties
allowed it to do so. Indeed, the Unionist party actively
contrived and encouraged it, in the hope of its own political
advantage. To the argument that a crisis situation over
Ireland developed because of the weakness and
incompetence of the Liberals, may be added the argument
that it came about because of the irresponsible and
unscrupulous ambitions of the Tories: 'Unionists, furious
with frustration at their continued exclusion from power,
were thus willing to adopt almost any means to defeat the
Liberals and return to office.' In their determination to
back Ulster, the Unionists were moved — as in 1886 — not by
the plight of Ulster itself, but by what Ulster could be
claimed to represent. As Bonar Law put it to a Belfast
audience in April 1912: 'Once again you hold the pass, the
pass for the empire . . . you will save the empire by your
example.'[4] This high-flown imperialist rhetoric may have
been genuine enough, but the greatest force behind English
Unionist support for Ulster was a sense of domestic outrage,
the belief that the Parliament Act of 1911, which ended the
Lords' veto, was the beginning of a revolutionary overthrow
of the world they knew and believed in. As Law put it in his
famous speech in 1912: 'We regard the government as a
revolutionary committee which has seized upon despotic
power by fraud.' In what he conceived as a desperate

---

[4] Law's extremism was equalled, if not exceeded, by that of Lord Milner. See
A.M. Collin, *Proconsul in Politics. A Study of Lord Milner in Opposition and in
Power* (London, 1963) pp. 183-215.

situation, Law was prepared if necessary to support the use of force by Ulster in order to overthrow this revolutionary committee which called itself a Liberal government. This was to employ an Irish weapon—armed Ulster intransigence—for an English party purpose, or to put the best interpretation on it, for an English constitutional purpose. But the narrow party motivation behind Unionist support for Ulster was made abundantly clear by Law's private willingness in October 1913 to arrange some kind of compromise settlement for Ireland when it became evident that unyielding Unionism might not be an electoral asset.

In the circumstances, it is hardly outlandish to conclude that not only was Ireland once again, in 1910-14, the victim of English party politics, but that Home Rule, far from being a fundamental issue between the English parties, was merely the battleground over which other matters—notably reform versus reaction—as well as the crude contest for party supremacy, were fought. Both parties, particularly after Gladstone, took an English not an Irish view of Home Rule. Both saw Ireland in an English and imperial context, which they proposed to maintain: their difference over Home Rule lay in their conflicting beliefs as to its re-percussions for the Union situation. The Liberals held that it would strengthen it, the Tories that it would destroy it. This was difference of means, not ends, a dispute over tactics. It was not sufficient a difference to account for the extraordinary dimensions of the crisis which overtook English political life in the period 1910-14. Nor was the actual Home Rule Bill anything more than a concession of limited local self-government. The profound con-vulsion that seized English politics at this time, ostensibly occasioned by Irish affairs, sprang in fact from sources deep within the evolution of England itself, multiple challenges of change—and decay—to that proud patrician world that reached its confident zenith in the 1890s.[5]

[5] This argument cannot be pursued here, but its elements may be traced in such books as George Dangerfield, *The Strange Death of Liberal England* (London, 1935); Barbara W. Tuchman, *The Proud Tower. A Portrait of the world before the War: 1890-1914* (London, 1966); Correli Barnett, *The Collapse of British Power* (London, 1972).

Whatever the responsibility of the Unionists for frustrating its implementation, the question remains open whether the kind of Home Rule planned by the Liberals in 1912–14 would have satisfied nationalist Ireland. Conservatism about their Irish policy was hardly less characteristic of the Liberals than of the Unionists. Even after 1916, as Dr D.G. Boyce observes, 'those sections of British opinion which were traditionally sympathetic to the cause of Irish self-rule had developed their ideas remarkably little beyond those of Gladstone's generation'. Indeed, since the death of that great man of principle, such sympathy had regressed. As the *Manchester Guardian* remarked in May 1918, there was 'a fundamental difference between Home Rule that is advocated, as Gladstone advocated the cause of Ireland, out of sympathy with a nationality that has been denied its just expression, and Home Rule conceded not in the ground of nationality but as a measure of improving the efficiency of collective government'. This latter was the basic impulse behind the third Home Rule Bill. Many if not most Liberals would have agreed with Lord Hugh Cecil's conservative stance in October 1918: 'We must accept the fact of Irish Nationality. It is regrettable, it is unhistorical; in view of Ulster's feeling it is even absurd. But it is a fact; the majority of Irishmen do think Ireland a nation and we must do the best we can in the circumstances.' Liberals were more prone to dwell on might have beens, than adjust to the realities of a new situation. Their response to the 1916 rebellion was a further illustration of that English tendency to take a righteous backward view of the Irish situation. As always, English politicians had the solution to Irish problems after they had reached crisis point: if only what they now advocated had been implemented before, the crisis would have been avoided. Therefore to implement it now would provide the solution — reasoning which utterly neglected the fact that the crisis had changed the situation. English efforts to pacify Ireland with the old Home Rule formula after the 1916 rebellion were out of keeping both with what was old and what was new in the Irish situation.

They represented however, a genuine English conviction that a settlement was urgently necessary for English reasons.

In the new post-1916 circumstances of Irish rebellion in the context of world war and American opinion, Ulster, once paraded as the bastion of the Empire, became an obstacle to that prompt settlement of the Irish question now regarded as imperative. Ulster's refusal to accept Home Rule led to partition, but, again, only because of the structure and exigencies of English politics. There were at least two obvious alternative procedures to deal with Ulster opposition — resort to coercion, or the calling of an election on the issue. Dr Buckland has made clear the vital role in this situation of political self-interest, and of the intransigence of Bonar Law: 'What, in fact, saved Ulster Unionism at this time was the attitude of Bonar Law . . . His support [for Sir James Craig's refusal to accept a Northern Ireland government subordinate to an all-Ireland parliament] made impossible any coercion of Ulster or any appeal to the country on the Ulster issue. Either course would have split the Unionist party in Great Britain and thus brought about the downfall of the coalition government.' Law was a persistent opponent of any conciliation of nationalist Ireland, and greatly influenced the thinking of Lloyd George. And so, the need to confront the Irish question was sacrificed to the continuance of the life of the coalition — a most serious national consideration in wartime, but this was in 1921 — and the issue evaded with the device of partition. This was not, as nationalist Ireland believed, what Britain wanted — both the government and public opinion were against it — but it was the only way to deal with the Irish question, given that Ulster intransigents had a stranglehold on the Unionist party in Britain.

The treatment of the twenty-six southern counties in 1921 was no less governed by the internal demands of British party politics, then in a state of flux and uncertainty because of the emergence in 1918 of a large Labour party. Maurice Cowling has pointed out that 'Lloyd George's primary aim during the treaty negotiations was not to find a formula for getting the Sinn Fein delegates to sign, but to ensure that whichever way the negotiations ended there would be a suitable political path available for him to follow'. That is, Lloyd George approached the Irish question not as a matter of isolated principle, but rather with a very keen sense of the context of English politics, and a wary eye to his own political future – or to use an Irish nationalist description, with 'a completely opportunist attitude'. It was very appropriate that he did so, because without his skill in winning and retaining support from the Conservatives in his coalition government, and his abilities in securing the reluctant acceptance of the Irish, the treaty negotiations would have collapsed, almost certainly in the direction of a more coercionist English policy in Ireland.

If the nature of Anglo-Irish relations fostered the Irish assumption that Ireland was a constant subject of English attention, the fact was that English politicians saw Ireland as merely part of their over-all responsibilities, and a sub-ordinate one at that. The misunderstanding and friction inherent in this situation was intensified by the English tendency to treat in a ruthlessly pragmatic, even cynical manner, what the Irish regarded as high principles: at a cabinet meeting in May 1921, Balfour urged Home Rule merely as a gambit to silence international criticism. At that time, when Ireland was on the threshold of self-determination, British politicians still viewed the Irish with contempt, still saw their behaviour as merely another manifestation of primitive violence, regarded them as 'an inferior race', 'children in politics and statesmanship', peasants, their leaders small men, their claims deserving condescension rather than recognition.

The politics of the relationship between England and Ireland offer a multitude of lessons, the most serious of which is that of the insufficiency of politics. Politics is not properly defined as being the art of the possible: too often its performance falls far short of the possible, and becomes the art of contriving stop gaps, of evasive action, of short-term problem solving, of minimum remedies. This kind of politics was the cause, historically, of much of Ireland's sickness. It became increasingly unlikely that the treatment which had produced the disease would also come up with the remedy. This was not only because of the constrictions placed on political action by the weight of tradition, which inhibited any new initiatives. It was also because of the very nature of politics. Politics is concerned with the present, and the immediate past. It cannot resolve history, and so, in the Irish case, was doomed to attend to contemporary symptoms rather than the ancient enduring disease.

Talk, public debate, is an essential element in the political process. In relatively normal situations, this may lead to decisions followed by effective action. In situations of crisis and conflict, particularly where there is a reservoir of divisive historical experience, debate tends to refer back to that experience and to reintroduce it into the political process. The past is thus brought alive and fought over again, to the detriment of the present. The past is full not only of crimes and bitterness, but of equally divisive ideals and myths, which are also well beyond any practical political resolution. Such was—and is—the Irish case, but its particulars may be related to general inadequacies in the political process as such. Public debate on contentious issues has an internal self-frustrating dynamic. Talk, because it permits the construction of theoretical solutions, acts as a generator of maximum expectations, if not utopian aims. Added to this, in complex, fragmented, and highly-charged situations, the construction of verbal solutions (which, given the extent of human ingenuity, and the range of opinions, soon exhausts the conceivable) prompts immediate criticism. This swiftly leads to a process of accelerating mutual attrition in which all possibilities of solution are explored, generate enemies, are vigorously attacked, and left as mangled casualties if not completely defunct. To allow a situation to develop in which there is no limitation to the possibilities which might be pursued in talk, is not only to generate partisanship in relation to all possibilities, but to invite the proliferation of such possibilities, in a way invariably anarchic and destructive. British policy in

Northern Ireland since 1968 is open to this criticism, which might be levelled more generally at policy since 1800: too much talk was permitted to precede too little action.

It is something of a principle of English democratic government that talk is ultimately capable of resolving all difficulties and differences and of producing workable agreement. This is not necessarily so: discussion may reveal that the standpoints of participants are much more in conflict than they were seen to be previously, and may be seriously provocative in revealing prejudice and hatred. Sociological analysis has shown that the peace and stability of society in Northern Ireland prior to 1968 was based on the mutual avoidance by Protestants and Catholics of any advertence to those matters on which they were divided: it was a society whose existence depended on a lack of fundamental communication. Opening up such communication destroyed that society. Furthermore, particularly in a very personalized society such as Ireland is, proposals and viewpoints are open to being judged not on their merits, but on an estimate of the character and known affiliations of their advocate. And the more prolonged and the more fundamental is discussion, the more likely is it to generate emotion, drift from essentials, raise side issues, and generally polarize participants.

At some crucial points in Anglo-Irish relations, and certainly recently, it might almost seem that the more talk the less possible it is to secure agreement, the more talk the more entrenched become traditional positions, the more talk the less progress is made away from the pre-existing historical determinants. If the Anglo-Irish treaty of 1921 seems to be an exception, it might be remarked that the cost was high — civil war for the Irish — that the talk was in the context of British willingness to resort again to force, and that, in any case, the talk resolved only the southern and easiest part of the difficulty. And what of the problem of those political forces which will not talk at all, and which yet remain vital factors in moving the situation?

A basic problem in Anglo-Irish relations has been that the English never recognized problems as basic, construing them only as questions of adjustments and administration. When at last compelled, in 1921, to admit that the relationship was beset by major problems, they still managed to avoid confronting them. By that time, such was the population and history of Ireland, that there was no solution of a kind which would please everyone, nor even one which would be tolerable to everyone. This stark reality was not recognized by English politicians who were seeking an immediate accommodation of the interests in conflict. The 1921 Treaty saw these elements juggled with the utmost political astuity by the Welsh wizard. First, the most resistant problem was lopped off and shelved — north-east Ulster. Then sufficient was conceded to the nationalist position to force realists into accepting this as all they could get at that time. Acceptance of limited concessions left the realists with the task of coping with the idealists and irreconcilable extremists in a civil war. The English tactic of getting Irish moderates to deal with Irish extremists was a hallowed one, certainly as old as the time of O'Connell.

The shortcomings of this tactic have only recently been revealed, for only since 1968 did it become obvious that the effect of the 1920-1 settlement was to relocate the Irish problem, reducing it from that of 32 counties to that of six. Its merit as an English tactic was that Irish moderates could not evade the role once bestowed: they would play it successfully or perish. However, the availability of this as a tactical possibility was dependent on the size of such potential forces of moderation. Political systems of the English type are dependent for their operation on the existence of a large moderate element in relation to very small extremist groups. A good deal of the political thinking — and hoping — about Northern Ireland has been dependent on this postulation, which is true of England, and of southern Ireland, but questionable in regard to the north. The outcome of the March 1974 general election in Northern Ireland was not encouraging to those whose potential solutions were based on the assumption that moderation existed and would eventually show itself decisively. The willingness of 'moderates' under extreme provocation to take up extreme positions is a lesson of European rather more than of English history, but it is a recurring theme of Anglo-Irish relations that the facts of Irish politics seldom conformed to what the English thought should occur.

Anglo-Irish relations have not yet escaped from the old routine of coercion and conciliation. In 1920-21 England left the coercion to the beneficiaries of the conciliation, both north and south. In the south, this eventually worked, though it was not until 1927 that the Republican opposition decided to participate in the Irish parliament, thus involving the whole people actively, for the first time, in the political process. This did not occur in the north. While the south eventually rid itself of the coercionist legacy, the north maintained it, and began to repeat within the confines of its own borders, the previous history of Anglo-Irish relations since 1800. In the north, the political, economic and social structure was latently — and sometimes actively — coercionist to a sufficient degree to ensure the passive acceptance of that structure by those opposed to it. Government without popular consensus is always possible so long as the absence of consensus is not expressed in massive violence or in crucial institutions. Once the lack of consensus is expressed in these areas, the classic English solution in the Irish context was repressive coercion accompanied by concessionary conciliation: this was the policy followed by the Northern Ireland government from 1968, though it took considerable British pressure to get that government to adopt its conciliatory aspect. The outcome was precisely what it had been when Britain had followed it, from 1800 to 1921. The concessions were made too slowly, grudgingly, and were inadequate. That they were made at all demonstrated the effectiveness of violence, and thus encouraged its continuance. Coercion was never sufficient to achieve repression, and bred hatred and fear. Social morality decayed and political life disintegrated.

It is a venerable witticism that the English never succeeded in answering the Irish question because the Irish were always changing the question. This points to a profound political truth: answers should anticipate questions. Solutions must not merely keep pace with the development of problems, but be in advance of that development, if they are to have any prospect of arresting it. The spectacle of solutions chasing problems and being rapidly outdistanced by them is a constant feature of Irish history. Precedent — the history of Irish land reform, or of the demand for Home Rule — plus the tendency of politics generally to make minimum responses to maximum challenges, call in question the assumption that normal political action is appropriate to those crisis situations which have arisen so frequently in Irish history. Normal political processes do not appear to be able to cope with problems of accelerating or rapid change, or of extreme community polarization.

This most serious inadequacy is evident in the slowness of parliamentary and legislative machinery, and in the fact that, of its nature, it exposes its proposed line of action to protracted public attention and debate. It is not suited to prompt action, nor to reducing the heat which may surround contentious issues. And the interruption of the political process by the intrusion of elections at vital moments is another factor. The election of June 1970 is, arguably, a case in point. James Callaghan contends that had he been able to continue his policy at that time, the chances of settlement in Northern Ireland were high, or, to make the negative point, the election result 'was a disaster for Northern Ireland. Not only were the initiatives we had intended not followed up, but the break in continuity came at the very worst time for the success of the struggle to prevent the Provisional IRA from capturing the sympathy of the minority'. Irish policy was affected by a British election in which Irish policy was hardly an issue.

Politicians are commonly charged with lack of vision: it is not a surprising failing in those whose main business is the here and now. The previous forty years were devoid of prophets of the Ulster disaster. Perhaps prophecy is more appropriately the duty of churchmen — one they have shirked — but Gladstone, in 1845, saw Ireland as the coming storm. Long-term prophecy has great potential political value, but even in the short term, vision, prediction even, is necessary for effective politics in immediate fast-moving situations. Unwillingness among effective politicians holding power to attempt to predict what will happen and to act accordingly, opens the road for anything to happen. To avoid prediction may seem proper in a politician, in view of the swiftly changing flow of events, and the openness of situations to be influenced by the unexpected, or even by total accidents. This certainly is a common English view. As Enoch Powell said, speaking on an Ulster theme in September 1968 '. . . there is a healthy instinct in British political parties to take account only of present issues and substantial opponents, and not to confer unmerited importance upon the ephemeral, the insignificant or the freakish'. If politics be taken up entirely with present concerns and what is currently substantial, it must leave itself totally unprotected against the future, and diminish its role to that of mere administration of what exists.

It is conceivable that a do-nothing, wait and see, political policy could be responsibly contrived, and be, in fact, a positive policy. When no action is possible without serious chance of grave error or uncontrollable consequences, it might be judged more prudent, the lesser of evils, to allow a complex crisis to evolve according to its own dynamics, in the hope that some intervention or some accident could precipitate a situation from which movement towards resolution was possible. This might be deemed a suspension of politics, but its deliberate adoption as a policy would be acknowledgement that a situation had passed beyond the political realm and was, for the present, beyond any political help. In Irish history such situations have been frequent enough. They have seldom borne any signs that they were anything other than testimony to political bankruptcy, the end result of carelessness, neglect, incompetence, and mal-administration.

5

The Economic Factor

BROADLY economic explanations of the disturbed history of Anglo-Irish relations have had a venerable history: they long predate Marx, and after Marx, were orthodox even in some of the most conservative areas of English thought. It was put to Robert Emmet in 1803 of the common people who had risen in rebellion with him that 'the object next to their hearts was a separation and a republic'. He replied: 'Pardon me, the object next to their heart was a redress of their grievances', and contended that if this could be secured peaceably 'they would prefer it infinitely to a revolution and a republic'. Later in the century this general interpretation became commonplace within Liberal, and, by the 1890s, within Tory circles: it took as obvious that the real dynamic behind Irish unrest and Irish nationalism was social and economic grievance, particularly rural poverty and the system of land tenure, not any genuine longing for political freedom or any real or widespread hatred of England. In consequence, socio-economic reform would pacify Ireland.

Was this conclusion justified? E.P. Thompson has written, in an English context: 'It is possible to detect in almost every eighteenth century crowd action some legitimizing notion . . . the men and women in the crowd were informed by the belief that they were defending traditional rights or customs; and, in general, that they were supported by the wider consensus of the community . . . [There was] a consistent traditional view of social norms and obligations, of the proper economic functions of several parties within the community, which taken together, can be said to constitute the moral economy of the poor. An outrage to these moral assumptions, quite as much as actual deprivation, was the usual occasion for direct action.'

Irish history affords ample illustration of this. It might be said that the Irish peasantry lived in a condition of permanent experience of moral outrage, given their continuing consciousness that the English had confiscated their land. This outrage was tolerable only under the threat of coercion, and if the landlords did not disturb the traditional economic sub-structures which existed beneath the English legal forms of ownership. In such circumstances, where peasant Ireland was wedded to old ways and deeply resistant to changing them, any form of attempted agrarian modernization was sure to encounter peasant resistance. So, Ireland's resistance to England in the nineteenth century, could well be interpreted, at least in part, as another instance of the classic universal reaction of archaism against modernization. It bears the classic features—the idea that the organic life of peasant and countryside is superior to the atomized and disintegratory world of modern science and modern urban civilization, the belief that the peasant's intimate attachment to the soil is the epitome of personal virtue and social stability, the peasant's conviction that far from being a radical or a revolutionary, he is seeking to defend or revive the hallowed and better way of life. The Irish peasant defence of the ways and values of the past against forces of change which would sweep these away drew on a moral economy wider and stronger than simple tradition: it was also sustained, in Ireland, by the power and authority of the church and priesthood which was part of the old order under the threat of change.

In view of all this, the English proposition that socio-economic reform would pacify Ireland—a proposition based on almost total unawareness of the beliefs and attitudes of the Irish peasant—was likely to prove quite false. Indeed, the precise opposite was the logical outcome: socio-economic reform would throw Ireland into violent turmoil. What the English saw as desirable improvements seemed to the Irish peasantry to promise the destruction of their entire life-style. What the Irish peasantry wanted by way of reform, seemed to the English totally revolutionary, so destructive was it of existing property rights and of current notions of progress: Irish archaism was so profound, so much at variance with English ideas of what should be, that it exhibited a most revolutionary complexion, especially in view of its violent expression. It was a confrontation in which both the English and the Irish saw each other as destructive revolutionaries.

The English idea that the causes of Irish unrest were economic and social (within a reformist English under-standing of those terms) tended to be at its strongest and most positive at times of relative quiet, and among those disposed to being interested in economics. In 1907 the director of the London School of Economics pronounced definitively: ' . . . the difficulties of Ireland are due to economic rather than religious or political causes.' Thomas Jones, professor of economics in Belfast in 1909, remarked later of his views at that time: '. . . I was not more blind than the statesman of the time in thinking that the economic problem was fundamental and would be decisive.' However, at times of crisis in Anglo-Irish relations the economic view tended to be replaced promptly by the political or the cultural, whereby the Irish were seen, not as agitated by dearth or mismanagement, but as in pursuit of a separation and a republic, or as anarchic barbarians by nature, not by environment. The economic interpretation of the Irish question accorded with the intellectual bias of the later nineteenth century, but it also had other advantages which led to its strong promotion by the more moderate Irish nationalist party. It was an explanation which avoided locating the problem in the nature of the Irish or in an extreme nationalism which incensed the English. Moreover, it placed the problem within the orbit of legislative remedy. It was an explanation which could be advanced in Ireland in terms of an indictment of England, and also neutralized for English consumption by blaming impersonal economic systems and laws. Nevertheless, the economic interpretation raised a point of fundamental disagreement between the English and the Irish: who or what was responsible for Ireland's woeful poverty?[1]

Economic reality—like absolute truth—eludes full discovery, and such parts as can be found are open to differing interpretation. Professor Noel Butlin has indicated the consequences of confusion and uncertainty for English—and Irish—economic history which flow from a statistical situation in which the United Kingdom was treated as one. The separation out of the Irish element, hardly yet begun, is imperative to the better understanding (indeed to any clear understanding at all) of the economic, social, and demographic history of the British Isles. This limitation understood, the central economic generalities appear to be as follows.[2] Nineteenth-century Ireland was an overwhelmingly agricultural economy, poor in resources, and backward in development. It was an economy both subservient to and dependent on the prosperous industrial economy of its British neighbour, and was thus subject to the two-fold fluctuations of a dependent economy, those within itself, and those within the economy on which it was dependent. Moreover it was an economy under pressures of change which have been termed 'modernization' and 'rural crisis'. It was in process of being transformed from intensive, subsistence, potato-centred cultivation into an economic pattern of larger holdings, the dominance of pasture farming, and greater prosperity, with the attendant social and demographic development of massive depopulation through emigration and later marriages. This picture is complicated by the economy's two-fold aspect—that of a maritime orientated commercial economy along the eastern coast, with substantial industrial development around Belfast, with a very different subsistence rural economy inland and to the west.

[1]. The various approaches to this question are summarized in Barbara Lewis Solow, *The Land Question and the Irish Economy, 1870-1903* (Cambridge, Massachusetts, 1971) pp. 2-4.

[2] For a summary of recent research see F. S. L. Lyons, *Ireland since the Famine*, pp. 34-70. See also Lee, *The Modernization of Irish Society*; L.M. Cullen, *An Economic History of Ireland since 1660* (London, 1972); L.M. Cullen (ed.) *The Formation of the Irish Economy* (Cork, 1969).

The central proposition to be taken from this, so far as Anglo-Irish relations were concerned, was that Ireland's was a poor and underdeveloped economy exhibiting many distressful signs: the question at issue was why? There is much to support Professor Cullen's judgement that 'The real determinants of Irish economic retardation . . . lay outside the legislative and . . . outside the fiscal sphere', and within the realm of basic economic facts and profound external economic changes—most importantly, within the overall consequences of being so close to the leader of the Industrial Revolution in a highly competitive and machine dominated age.[3] This is to stress the direct economic consequences, but perhaps of no less significance was the way in which the Industrial Revolution diminished, constricted, and diverted English understanding of what was happening in Ireland. It might be argued that it was, above all, the Industrial Revolution which drove England and Ireland irrevocably apart, for as a consequence of that Revolution within England, England and Ireland became two differing worlds, each unintelligible and hostile to the other.

The farmland enclosures in Britain which preceded and accompanied the Industrial Revolution, together with the rapid development of an urban industrial economy, effectively eliminated the peasant question from domestic English politics. It also substantially diminished the forces of agrarian conservatism in England, so that they came to consist of a landed upper class, without a basis in mass peasant support. In these circumstances, the vast peasant question which Ireland posed seemed to English legislators and commentators, concerned with very different problems of their own, anachronistic, irrelevant, and essentially

[3] For an illuminating detailed case study relating to the Irish land question, see W. A. Maguire, *The Downshire Estates in Ireland 1801-1845. The management of Irish landed estates in the early nineteenth century* (Oxford, 1972). This provides a useful corrective to the traditional nationalist depiction of the agrarian situation, not only in suggesting a greater degree of awareness among some landlords of their social obligations, but in explaining the circumstances in which landowners found themselves: 'what does seem clear is this: serious economic and social problems existed, of a sort that landowners were not primarily responsible for creating, and with which even the most sympathetic of them could not adequately deal'. (p. 247).

unreal. Within Britain, the peasant question — to be so troublesome later in other modernizing states — had been largely avoided because the peasantry had been absorbed as the manpower for industrialization. This could not obtain in Ireland, though Irish emigration to Britain was a form of this process. The result was that, given that the peasant question had solved itself in Britain, English governments lacked experience in dealing with it, failed to understand its nature, and gravely underestimated its importance and intractability. Seen thus, the Irish question in the nineteenth century was England's peasant question. Conflict was unavoidable in that England was the agent of a modernizing process necessarily directed against the old agrarian order of primitive subsistence farming, but the way in which England handled it greatly worsened the difficulty.

First, there was the matter of the long unresolved continuance of the confrontation between the new ways and the old. Had modernization taken place with the rapidity experienced in Britain itself, the conflict may not have become so embedded, so ridden with impatience and exasperation on the one side, and with yearnings to return to an idealized past on the other — and also so disposed to attract (or create) other levels and forms of difference. In 1881 Cardinal Newman observed that '. . . the question between the countries is not one of land or property, but of *union*'. No doubt that is what it was in the 1880s, but whether it would have come to that given an earlier answer to questions of land and property is another matter. The slowness of the modernization process reflects both Irish and English factors. The sheer size of the peasant problem, both in terms of actual numbers and of its dominant place in the Irish economy, militated against any rapid radical treatment. In any case, the English government was not disposed to confront it, both for reasons of lack of interest and understanding, and because of the fact that Irish government rested on the landlord élite. This dependence made intervention in the economy both difficult and potentially dangerous. It also saddled England with such odium as might arise from grievances against landlords. Many of these landlords relied on British power to sustain a system not merely anachronistic or exploitative, but gravely provocative of unrest. They did not modernize, nor did they discharge a traditional role. The traditional relationships could not endure or remain stable where the landlord's contribution to the welfare of Ireland, or to his immediate locality, did not exist, or could not be seen, where such a landlord persisted in pressing for dues when justification was not evident. Landlords who were exceptions to this general rule certainly existed, but these fell mainly into the category of well-intentioned modernizers who generated often violent traditionalist resistance which they could not understand. Peasant conceptions of social justice were based on the belief that each element in society must discharge its duties before it could claim its rights. In Ireland, not only the absentee landlord, but the system whereby tenants did not possess any improvements they made, were glaring injustices, from the peasants' viewpoint, as were changes in tenure and production associated with economic modernization. The circumstances of government involvement — or failure to intervene — together with the efforts of doctrinaire nationalists, translated the conflict between landlord and peasant into one between England and Ireland, so that the relationship between the two countries was often seen — by both — as the landlord-peasant relationship writ large.

In the 1820s and 30s, and in the 70s and 80s, peasant revolution was in the air in Ireland. At both times, such was the ability of the dominant Irish politicians — O'Connell and Parnell — that peasant violence was largely sublimated into political pressure, and given the dressing of a nationalist ideology. Had the famine not destroyed the earlier movement, or had reform removed or weakened the basis of peasant grievances, the Irish question in its peasant aspect might have demanded, and received, a much earlier resolution — or have died away. As it was, the level at which an unremedied peasant discontent was sustained throughout the nineteenth century was below that of compelling England to attend to it as something urgent and inescapable, while being sufficient to provide the basis and mass dynamic for a nationalist political movement which eventually could not be denied.

Britain's involvement with the landowning ascendance in Ireland was not only a political liability. It was also a committal to an ultimately intolerable reactionary economic position. The flow of economic development in Britain itself was against the power of the landed élite, and towards the power of the commercial and industrial middle classes. Transferred to Ireland, this process drastically weakened British power, for the middle classes were both very weak, and Irish, and power drifted into popular nationalist hands. The eventual repudiation by Britain of support for the reactionary landed élite placed Britain in the position of having both tolerated the continued unsettlement of the Irish peasantry and then having refused to maintain the structure which both provoked and contained that unsettlement. Britain successively sustained the worst aspects of a disintegrating economic landlord order, and encouraged similarly disintegratory policies of economic modernization, and all at the same time as making grudging concessions to reactionary peasant demands. The outcome was a mass of economic and political policy contradictions and fragmentation, a virtually certain recipe for turmoil.

There were other socio-political implications deriving from the differing economic characters of the two countries. Ireland, lacking a vigorous and independent class of affluent town dwellers, was weak in the area of the source of the usual aggressive bourgeois demands for a voice in government, and particularly in the control of finance. Indeed the Irish were hostile to the whole spirit of urban life, so well developed in England and Europe. Of this Sean O'Faolain has written: 'We have always feared towns. We have felt them as spearheads of lifeways which are complex, troublesome and challenging'. It was, from ancient times, a land of isolated holdings. Its economic character deprived Ireland of the particular kind of bourgeoisie so important in colonial and nationalist movements elsewhere. One effect of the absence of such a class was, perhaps—as some Englishmen believed in the 1830s—to unstabilize Irish society by making more obvious and bitter than would otherwise have been the case, the gulf between property and poverty. More certainly, the weakness of the Irish bourgeoisie had important implications in areas where leadership might have been exercised. The absence of an entrepreneurial class (save in north-east Ulster) meant that Ireland lacked economic initiative and leadership coming from within, and this was certainly one factor making for economic stagnancy. The Irish professional and commercial classes, dependent as they were on English patronage and connections, tended, at least until late in the nineteenth century, to be subservient to Britain and to lack any independent life of their own. The radical political class, to the extent that there was one above the level of the peasantry, tended to be the lower bourgeoisie, or rather, some members of it, and their coherence was a fitful one. This situation weakened Irish political life generally, as well as the nationalist movement in particular. Looking considerably higher in the social scale, Ireland's poverty could also be seen as having repercussions in diminished leadership and public activity.

It might be that a richer Ireland would have challenged England sooner and more successfully. 'Why was Ireland poor?' therefore becomes a question which relates not only to the matter of the living conditions of Irishmen, but also to their political conditions. Was this poverty simply the outcome of the hard facts of economic life, or had the English government neglected, deliberately or through stupidity or incompetence, its responsibility to stimulate economic growth? 'In practical terms, the government, the most powerful potential agent of economic development in Irish circumstances, simply opted out in obeisance to dogmas originally promulgated on the basis of English conditions. In the final analysis it was less the lack of mineral than of mental resources that inflicted on Ireland the slowest rate of growth of national income in western

Europe . . . between 1848 and 1914.'

This recent judgement by Dr Joseph Lee, provides an entrée to the world of Irish economic imagery, for its core is the proposition that the Irish economy was within English control, but the English failed to attend to it. Whether the English attended to it or not can be investigated, and the evidence indicates that they did not, but the importance of this neglect as a factor in the total economic situation lies in the field of speculation, not that of calculation. The Irish nationalist view took it as basic that England was to blame for Irish economic retardation and usually attributed this to deliberate design, rather than neglect. This image was not based on economic research, any more than could be the contention that retardation derived from the character and personality of Ireland, particularly its strong rural tradition. Rather was it an image related to propaganda and political purposes. Just as it suited Unionists to attribute economic stagnancy to the nature of the Irish, it suited nationalists to trace it to Ireland's political subjection. Each of these interpretations tended to adjust its picture of the economy to support its political argument. Unionists were capable of describing the economy as prosperous and buoyant when they were contending that Home Rule was a very narrowly based and transitory demand: this was the positive case for the continuance of English rule. The negative case was that English rule prevented the economy from becoming even more regressive and sluggish than it already was. Nationalists consistently advanced the sombre interpretation: exaggeration of Irish poverty and depression was a major theme of the nationalist depiction of the Irish economy. The end of English rule could then be promoted as the end of stark exploitation and the beginning of an age of plenty and prosperity.

Superficially, the nationalist interpretation seemed to accord with the facts. Ireland's economic decline and most massive problems followed the Union: it was therefore tempting to suppose that this was caused by the Union. Similarly, rural poverty to the degree of famine existed under a particular type of land system: this system was obviously the cause. The seizing of simple and obvious factors as fundamental causes drew attention away from basic economic problems, and issued in a utopian view of Ireland's economic future: get rid of English rule, and landlords, and prosperity would blossom forth.

This type of thinking was consistently evident. Evictions were attributed in Ireland to landlord greed and malignancy whereas the more frequent cause was often the impact of agricultural depression on the financial position of landlords. The 'Land War' of the 1870s and 1880s was taken as proof of the depths of landlord-contrived peasant desperation, whereas it is certainly arguable that it derived from improved peasant status, a revolution of rising expectations. What is certain is that basic economic developments and fluctuations had profound political consequences for the relationship between England and Ireland, either directly, or, more often, through being interpreted as English or landlord contrivances. And it is also certain that the effect of these developments and fluctuations was little recognized, and that both Irish and English reformers believed that matters related to land tenure were at the root of all Irish economic difficulties.

The existence of this belief in England is attested to by a history of defeated bills and some actual legislation, beginning with the 1870 Land Act. Its validity was confirmed for English reformers by the fact that the belief was shared by the Irish. From the 1850s the major spokesmen of Ireland hammered away at land tenure as being the major trouble, and reform of it the remedy to Ireland's ills. Barbara Solow, who holds this analysis to have been false, explains the continuance of the Irish land agitation and the English response as illustration of the proposition that 'when an inadequate policy fails to produce results, it is applied in even stronger doses'. It was a fixation which, according to R.D. Collinson Black, had adverse economic consequences. 'The problems of landownership often seemed, in Ireland . . . to occupy public attention to the exclusion of any consideration of improving the agriculture which might take place on the land.' This was true: funds for agricultural development were quite inadequate, and so was initiative. But the reasons for this do not lie entirely within the realm of English neglect. In one of its aspects, an improving English policy was bound up completely with the necessity for a prior resolution of the tenure matter. That English view which saw farming on the English model, capitalist farming, as the solution to Ireland's problems was based, for its practical implementation, on sweeping away the vestiges of traditional tenures. And, from the opposite standpoint, of reasserting those traditions, the Irish themselves insisted on prior attention to the tenure matter. Agricultural improvement ran a very poor second in their land reform programme and Irish farming was to prove strongly resistant to the introduction of improving methods. To the Irish peasant, ownership—the emotional or moral question—was far more important than production—the economic question

In Ireland, the thesis of English exploitation was greatly strengthened from the 1870s by the appearance of a number of important historical works of a polemical kind and by tracts and even official reports which furthered this account of the relationship in its economic aspect. The seemingly authoritative character of this material was heightened by the fact that its authorship was substantially English and Anglo-Irish, culminating in the conclusion by the Financial Relations Commission in 1896 that Ireland had been overtaxed. Naturally, all this was most welcome to nationalist propagandists. The fact that economic arguments, with their trappings of statistics and impressive jargon, appeared to add a scientifically demonstrable and objective dimension to nationalist polemic encouraged their greater use. Besides, the economic was a ground on which all Irishmen might be united against England: it cast all Irishmen as the victims of a common exploitation, thus abstracting from differences of religion and class. Nor did the argument of economic exploitation necessitate embracing socialism—the relatively well-off Irish could be depicted as victims as well as the very poor.

Naturally this was an interpretation of the relationship particularly congenial to Marxists. Writing from Ireland in May 1856, Engels told Marx: 'By consistent oppression they have been artificially converted into an utterly impoverished nation and now, as everyone knows, fulfil the function of supplying England, America, Australia, etc., with prostitutes, casual labourers, pimps, pickpockets, swindlers, beggars and other rabble.'

Marx himself, in a comment which might equally well have come from John Mitchel, wrote, 'In 1855-66, 1,032,644 Irishmen were displaced by 996,877 head of cattle', and Lenin observed that 'Britain owes her "brilliant" economic development and the "prosperity" of her industry and commerce largely to her treatment of the Irish peasantry . . .'

It might be assumed that all this would have been music to Irish ears, had they been aware of what Marxists were saying, but they were not, until James Connolly began to preach Marxism to a hostile Ireland from the late 1890s. However, the founders of Marxism were not interested in Ireland for its own sake—it was a near perfect example of 'the idiocy of rural life' blended with that opiate of the people, religion. They were interested in Ireland as a case supporting their central theories, and as potential support for a proletarian revolution in Britain, and they regarded the Irish with a very bourgeois contempt for the degraded products of exploitation. It took Connolly, and after him Jim Larkin, to attempt to relate Marxism sympathetically to the Irish situation. In practice this attempt was unsuccessful, because it went against the two most powerful forces in Ireland, nationalism and Catholicism, but in theory, at least two aspects of the Marxist position harmonized with salient features of the nationalist tradition—its stress on unity, and its challenge to oppression and exploitation.

At the time Connolly set out the Marxist message, nationalism and Catholicism monopolized the ideological ground in Ireland and there was room only for Connolly and those few who thought like him to attach themselves as appendages to the forces of nationalism. But the shortcomings of the nationalist achievement after 1921 meant that the Marxist message retained a relevance to the Irish situation more particular than whatever generalized relevance Marxism might claim to have in any human society. The nationalist achievement was defective in several important respects. Ireland remained divided, and remained, however politically free, economically subject to England. And political freedom had not brought, internally, prosperity or social justice. On the matter of continued disunity, it could be contended that if nationalism had failed to unify Ireland, because of the sectarian division, socialism would unify it because it abstracted from that division and would thus overcome it. In so far as prosperity and social justice were concerned, if nationalism had not achieved these as a by-product, then socialism would, because that was socialism's direct objective.

After 1921, English commercial presence in Ireland remained strong and obvious, continued support for Connolly's argument that socialism was a pre-condition to complete freedom. Socialism then, had a direct relevance to the central ideals of Irish nationalism—complete unity, and complete freedom. The continued failure to achieve these nationalist ideals through nationalism, was the main impetus behind the survival of the socialist tradition in Ireland, and its more recent substantial revival.

But the basic obstacle to class unity—religious and cultural differences—had already been revealed in the relations between the British and Irish working classes, as well as between Protestant and Catholic workers within Ireland. British trade unions consistently endeavoured to avoid Irish issues, but when they were compelled to confront them, they refused to support the Irish position. This reflected not only British prejudice, but the difficulty of coping with an Irish working class divided between Unionists and Home Rulers, and influenced by a vigorously anti-socialist Irish Catholicism. The failure of the English working class to interest itself in, or support the grievances of Irish workers was not entirely disadvantageous to the Irish nationalist cause: the English establishment was never confronted by the alliance it feared most — Ireland and the English labour movement. It seems likely that such an alliance would have frightened away from Irish causes those bourgeois liberals and nationalists who did so much to advance them.

Some English intellectuals accepted the Irish nationalist proposition that Ireland was the victim of English exploitation, but the general English view of the economic aspects of the relationship was quite other than this. A first question in assessing the conflict between Irish and English economic opinions and prejudices is whether or not the English were aware of the realities of Irish economic life, and of the condition of the country from time to time. Ernst Strauss, among others, has claimed: 'Ignorance of the facts was not one of the causes of Irish misery during the nineteenth century. The average number of parliamentary committees or commissions of inquiry into the state of Ireland was in the neighbourhood of five every year, at least during the first half of the nineteenth century . . .' This claim has been contested by Dr Lee, who sees it as confusing information with mere opinions, opinions which were virtually useless as guides to policy making. He argues that the government lacked basic or adequate socio-economic information, and in any case was not disposed to attend to what information was available. There is ample evidence that British experts had distorted and erroneous impressions of Ireland's socio-economic situation. In the early 1860s J.S. Mill believed that Ireland was prosperous and contented. This he attributed to the Encumbered Estates Act of 1849, and held that Ireland's only real remaining grievance was the Anglican established church. In this Mill demonstrated not only his ignorance, but other characteristics of English opinion — an astonishingly superficial optimism about Ireland when it was quiet (the reverse was a black and bitter despair when it was unquiet) and a tendency to explain any improvement in the Irish economy as produced by the most

recent previous piece of relevant English legislation. This
latter tendency was particularly curious as, according to the
classical economic orthodoxy of the day, such government
intervention was a departure from best economic practice.
Mill's standpoint illustrates also the English assumption that
Ireland would be humoured by legislative gestures,
demonstrating some English sympathy towards Irish
sentiment, short of substantial concessions. However, Mill
was to confess to the House of Commons in February 1866
that he had been quite wrong:

'We were present at the collapsing of a great delusion.
England had for a considerable number of years been
flattering itself that the Irish people had come to their
senses, that they had got Catholic Emancipation and the
Incumbered Estates Bill, which were the only things they
could possibly want; and had become aware that a nation
could not have anything to complain of when it was under
such beneficient rulers . . .'

Mill's acknowledgement of the gravely defective character
of English understanding hardly affected the central
propositions in the general English assessment. There
remained a strong and continuing conviction that
Ireland was poor and backward, and distracted, because of
the nature of the Irish as a people. It was believed that the
alleged personal characteristics of the Irish—their idleness,
want of thrift, and the like—meant that they had neither
the qualities nor the inclination to throw off their poverty.

The poverty of Ireland aroused all the prejudices bourgeois England held generally in relation to the poor—that
their repulsive condition was due to their own fault,
through an inferior nature, or sin. Even the basic features
of the Irish economy aroused English prejudice and
distaste. Walking through Wales, George Borrow exclaimed
'On my right was a field of oats; on my left a Methodist
chapel—oats and Methodism! What better symbols of
poverty and meanness!' In Ireland it was oats and
Catholicism. The prejudices of men whose idea of rural life
was formed by the orderly English lowlands, with their
wheat fields and tidy villages, were affronted by the rough

and restless ways of Ireland, where kinship counted more than contract and where the magical and the practical blended in habits repugnant to English taste. Radically divergent values and habits led the English to assess the Irish as dirty, and wedded both to their poverty and primitive ways of life. The English mind calculated worth in terms of material resources, and of progress and change. On this scale the Irish rated very low indeed. Their wealth was in spiritual values, and they were simply not interested in progress and change as understood by the English. Indeed in the central area of economy, the land, they exhibited stubborn conservatism, rejecting improvements in order to maintain primitive and unproductive farming methods. However, all of this, far from presenting to England the image of an Ireland uninterested in the things of this world, transmitted the opposite, the image of a grasping parasitic cunning. Lloyd George, for instance, believed that the Irish were greedy beyond any other part of the United Kingdom, a conclusion he derived from experience as Treasurer. In the cabinet discussions of 1920–21, he was adverting constantly to what he saw as the Irish desire to evade its share of the war debt and of taxation, and to continue to live off Britain. There is no doubting a widespread Irish conviction that England owed Ireland financial recompense for centuries of exploitation and that individual Irishmen, and Ireland generally, had an entitlement to recoup this debt as best they could—through tax evasion, social services, repudiation of obligations, or whatever means came to hand.

The main area of Irish economic grievance, as it became outspoken towards the end of the nineteenth century, was situated in the past—particularly in regard to the eighteenth century when, it was claimed, England had deliberately destroyed Irish commerce and industry, and the first half of the nineteenth when, it was alleged, England had allowed Ireland to be overcome by the calamity of famine. These were times when English policy was dictated by the belief that the world of economics was governed by immutable laws and principles, which could be transgressed only at great peril, and, in any case, were operative above any effort to adjust them. It was held that these laws always operated to long-term economic betterment, whatever transitory disruption or difficulty they might entail. These basic economic principles were that nothing should impede the free operation of economic forces, such as supply and demand, that untrammelled private enterprise was the source of all healthy economic development, and that the state should never interfere in the sphere of economics—in all, *laissez faire*. These ideas amounted to an economic enshrinement of the principle of the survival of the fittest. Ireland was unfit.

It was a common Irish conviction that these economic guidelines were aimed deliberately against Ireland. This was not so. They were generalizations drawn from experience, that of English trade and commerce followed by the Industrial Revolution, in which private enterprise, competition, and lack of regulation had produced wealth and power. This experience was not merely irrelevant to the Irish situation, it was inimical to it. Ireland's poverty neither generated nor attracted the kind of individual initiative blessed under *laissez faire*: the only hope of economic improvement, state initiative, encouragement and protection, was ruled out as bad economic practice. It has been held that 'The government's failure to stimulate economic growth was due more to intellectual irresponsibility than to political ill-will'. Deliberate contrivance may be discounted—though some Englishmen took obvious pleasure in seeing these laws work to Ireland's discomfort—but if 'intellectual irresponsibility' be a valid way of describing the doctrines of *laissez faire*, then this worked to the misery of more than Ireland. Working class England was also its victim, that other nation of Disraeli's *Sybil*. Disraeli's Chartist speaks of: 'Two nations between whom there is no intercourse and no sympathy; who are as ignorant of each others' habits, thoughts and feelings, as if they were dwellers in different zones or inhabitants of different planets, who are formed by a different breeding, are fed by a different food, one ordered by different manners, and are not governed by the same laws.'

This could have been an account of the relationship between England and Ireland: it was, of course, in reference to the rich and the poor in England. Eventually, the state was compelled to invade increasingly the domain of *laissez faire*, to curb and cushion its harsh operation, not merely in regard to Ireland, but as it affected England's *other* other nation, the poor. But to the Irish, unable to see any problems other than their own, the classical principles of English economy seemed aimed at the degradation of them alone.

These principles also had important effects on attitudes within the relationship. The belief that sacrosanct economic laws existed was dangerous because it encouraged the assumption that what was actually taking place in an economy was in conformity with those laws. So it was that the English were able to view as quite natural and ultimately beneficial what was experienced by the Irish as misery and disaster, even death. The impact of such an apparently inhuman set of judgements on Irish opinion was traumatic. To assess the famine, as so many Englishmen did, as an event which, however dreadful, had brought about necessary and progressive socio-economic changes, seemed to the Irish to show a disregard for proper values so complete as to be barbaric. To regard emigration in the same light seemed a similar example of English malevolence and inhumanity.

The importance of emigration in poisoning Anglo-Irish relations needs stressing. Not only did it set up a hostile and powerful Ireland in America, it sustained an enduring sense of grievance and clash of values. It was a common English argument that Irish poverty (the cause of all Irish discontent and unrest) sprang from rural over-population and uneconomic holdings. Population needed to be reduced, holdings consolidated, and progressive farming organization and techniques, together with British capital, introduced. Anything which might effect this, such as famine which would induce emigration, must be a good thing, however painful in the short term. This English economic logic encountered the obstruction of major socio-political facts in practice, for it was coupled with the reasonable conclusion that the only way to attract British capital and initiative, and permit better farming, was the establishment of a climate of security and confidence. The proposition has a familiar modern ring, being frequently encountered in its application to the current situation in Northern Ireland, and still, as in the nineteenth century, tending to produce coercionist conclusions. However, the logic was circular and self-defeating. Poverty produced discontent and unrest, but this unrest produced the conditions which made it impossible to establish the remedies for poverty.

The fact that the English analysis was correct in terms of modern economic development was irrelevant. The famine assisted modernization by destroying the subsistence economy and allowing its replacement by production for the market. So did emigration. In so far as Ireland was in fact overpopulated in terms of its then resources and opportunities, emigration was a humane process benefiting those who went and those who stayed: such was a usual English argument. And emigration, in so far as it allowed for upward social mobility, for Irishmen to achieve prosperity and positions inconceivable in their own society, might be seen as socially healthy, providing an outlet for social dynamism. It was also a process which, through remittances from overseas, provided a substantial injection of money into the Irish economy as well as improving individual living standards.

None of this was accepted in the Irish image of emigration. The English image focused mainly on its economic benefits, the Irish image fastened on its social and national costs. The Irish image was one of human affliction, personal calamity, a draining of family and national substance, and an undermining of the whole Irish way of life. In this view, the English favoured emigration as a means of weakening the Irish people, and eventually of driving them out of their own country entirely. British newspapers, especially *The Times*, offered assessments of emigration which supported this conclusion. In 1851, the places of peasants cleared from estates in Mayo were being taken by Scottish farmers. The *Glasgow Herald* remarked 'If the country continued to be thinned . . . we may yet have the power, so much desiderated, of establishing a British population in Ireland and rendering real the Union of the United Kingdom'. Later, in phrases of nationalist agitation, when British observers saw emigration as a safety valve for revolutionary tendencies, Irish nationalists saw it as a weakening of their movement. More generally, in terms of the economy, Irish nationalists came to argue that emigration was not an effect of the backward Irish economy, it was a cause of it. If all the human resources that Ireland had been compelled to export had been retained, Ireland's progress and wealth and power and prestige — and independence — would have been great indeed. So the enduring grievance of emigration provided a context not only for blaming the English for what existed, and for their efforts to destroy the old life ways, but for accusing England of depriving Ireland of the achievement of all the visionary ideals and might-have-beens of greatness which fertile nationalist imaginations could invent.

The damage which these images did to the relationship is incalculable. The direct practical consequences of England's adherence to its own economic orthodoxy in dealing with Ireland are more readily weighed. Until the late 1860s — and possibly this was already too late to admit remedy — the cause of Irish land reform was confronted in England by unanimous opposition. The intractability of the landed class was supported by the middle class liberals and even radicals who saw in the sanctity of property and freedom of contract the fundamental foundations of prosperity and social improvement. In 1832 Francis Place observed in relation to Ireland, 'I do not consider that a state of civilization in which property is not secure.' This comment illuminates not only the value put on respect for property, but a basic reason why many Englishmen regarded the Irish as uncivilized — they had no respect for English notions of property. It was a line of reasoning which led naturally to coercion as being morally justifiable in Ireland in the interests of progress towards civilization.

How central an article of English faith were the orthodox laws of property was revealed by the consternation and hostility provoked by J.S. Mill's criticism of that faith in his *England and Ireland*, in 1868. 'Every man should make up his mind' admonished *The Times*, 'whether the received laws of property are to be upheld in the United Kingdom; or whether, beginning first with Ireland, we are to establish principles which will unsettle our whole social fabric . . .' Although Mill's views were attacked as virtual advocacy of communism, they were in fact highly conservative. *England and Ireland* was intended to vindicate the Union, endangered, he believed, by England's failure to concede agrarian reform. After condemning England's defects in imagination and action in regard to Ireland in the past, Mill urged agrarian reform on several grounds. It was necessary as an act of justice, it would remove the basis for revolutionary nationalism, it would satisfy the criticism or consciences of English liberals and democrats, and would conciliate international opinion. But Mill's arguments did not persuade England to accept Irish land reform. Fenianism did that. As always, argument — even that of prominent Englishmen — was insufficient. The threat of agrarian revolution disposed parliament to think in terms of reform.

One of Mill's themes had been that England's past treatment of Ireland had been blameworthy. This confession of error became a constant note from the 1870s on, in the most influential and popular English and Anglo-Irish writing on the relationship, Froude and Lecky in particular. In 1903 this judgement was accepted in the first scholarly study of the economic aspects of the relationship, Alice Murray's *A History of the Commercial and Financial Relations Between England and Ireland from the Period of the Restoration*, in which all Ireland's ills were traced to England's commercial policies.

'. . . the commercial policy of England affected the economic condition of Ireland . . . by throwing the mass of the people on the land, aggravated the later agrarian troubles . . . this same commercial policy, combined with the Penal Laws, caused a grievous deterioration of the national character, to which even the present poverty and backwardness of Ireland may be traced . . . the effect of the restrictions placed by England on Irish trade and commerce . . . are still with us, and may be seen partly in the actual condition of the people, partly in their heritage of hatred to the law, and suspicion of England.'

Such conclusions testify to the acceptance, even among English analysts, of the Irish nationalist economic interpretation. Why this acceptance? Firstly, it was confined largely to liberal intellectual circles where sensitive consciences and self-criticism were in vogue. The more hard-headed, like the Duke of Argyll who conceded that 'the diseased condition of the country is due in some measure to these old sins of England' were firmly 'against sitting in perpetual sackcloth and ashes' because of that. Still others—the majority of English public men—found Gladstonian acknowledgement of a debt owed Ireland by England for past injustices, incomprehensible or ridiculous. So, such acknowledgements of exploitation as there were, were limited to the few. Those few found the nationalist economic interpretation an obvious and convenient explanation of a self-evident fact. England was rich, Ireland was poor. England ruled Ireland. Therefore England must be responsible for Ireland's poverty. But, happily for the liberal mind, the explanatory emphasis of this interpretation was located in the eighteenth century or the early nineteenth. It was therefore possible to exonerate the present, and to locate the blame in times and attitudes long gone by. Ireland might be placated with the assurance that these old sins had now been discovered, and that the generous and perceptive remedial measures of the present would soon dispose of that unfortunate legacy. Mistakes there had been—and some moral satisfaction and comfort might be taken in acknowledging them—but this was all over. If the Irish would be reasonably patient, recognizing that all the errors could not be remedied instantly, all would be adjusted eventually to mutual satisfaction. Blaming one's predecessors had the advantage of their not being able to defend themselves, and of placing oneself in the favourable light of having such superior insight as enabled the discovery and remedying of their mistakes. Such would appear to have been the mood of such English liberals as were concerned about Ireland in the early twentieth century. Had Ireland's problems and Ireland's impatience been confined to the sphere governed by economics, perhaps the economic measures of the 1890s and early 1900s, both in what they did and the understandings they exemplified, might have settled the Irish question.

6

Catholics and Protestants

IN relation to Ireland, Robert Malthus is usually associated with the doctrine of overpopulation and the dogmatism of the then new political economy. However, it is outside that economic realm, and in regard to the assessment of religious prejudice, that his perceptions seem most acute. He wrote in the *Edinburgh Review* in 1808:

'If it be really true, that the middling and lower ranks of society in this country are by no means prepared to consider the Irish Roman Catholics as fellow Christians worshipping the same God, and fellow subjects entitled to the same civil privileges; if they are really so bigoted as to wish to deny the benefits of the British constitution to about a fourth part of the population of the empire, and so ignorant as to imagine they can do it with safety, the evil admits of no other remedy than that of bringing the subject repeatedly before them — of familiarizing them to a more just and rational consideration of it — and of endeavouring to work into their minds the conviction, that, in holding such opinions, they are not only violating the genuine spirit of Christianity, but blindly endangering their own security, and risking the subjugation or dismemberment of the empire.'

In both its penetration and its tone this comment was most unusual. Much more typical of the time was the complaint made to the Chief Secretary of Ireland during the 1807 elections that whiskey and the exhortations of priests — evils of equal degradation — had whipped the 'popish mob' into a frenzy. A salient feature of Ireland's image as Englishmen saw it, was that of violent peasant politics controlled by priestcraft: Englishmen never thought in terms of their own politics being in any way clerically influenced, despite the importance of the episcopal element in the House of Lords. As seen by Englishmen, and Protestants in Ireland, clerical influence in politics was malign for a variety of powerful reasons. In the earlier nineteenth century it was seen to represent a threat to the health of the constitution in that it challenged the vital principle that members of parliament should not be dictated to by their constituents. No inconsistency was seen in the English and Irish Protestant willingness to accept, and encourage, landowner influence in politics. Landowners were held to have legitimate rights and interests in politics, whereas the priesthood did not. And the priesthood had the unfair advantage of being able to back its influence with threats of eternal punishment: the landlords could avail themselves merely of the terrors of this world.

More basically, the power of the priesthood in Ireland was deplored because it seemed detrimental to the interests of the country—a conclusion also reached by some Irishmen. It was held that this power attempted to distort national opinion and action to suit its own interests and purposes which were, generally, the aggrandizement of the Roman Catholic Church and, particularly, the inflation of the clergy's own role in Irish life. To the English mind, steeped in a tradition where the church was subject to the state, and where, by convention, parish clergy did not appear to intrude into the sphere of politics, the Irish situation—where bishops were active in political affairs on the national level, and priests no less active in their localities—seemed a gross disorder in the body politic. Ireland presented a scene in which the hierarchies of politics deemed proper by Englishmen were being, apparently, stood on their heads. And what was much worse, this aberration was working towards the furtherance of objectives totally reprehensible to the English mind—Irish nationalism and Roman Catholicism. While their religion by its mere existence aroused all the suspicion, fear, and prejudice produced by Romanism in the English mind, the prominence of the clergy in Irish nationalist politics gave this an intensity and immediacy which made the threat of priestcraft seem a major dangerous element in the Irish situation.

It was certainly a fact that the clergy and the Catholic religion were major determinants in Irish life and politics.[1] But the English and Protestant reaction neglected the powerful limitations that existed on the church's role in public affairs. There was, first and foremost, the ideological conservatism of the nineteenth-century church, reinforced by its harsh treatment by nationalists, liberals and socialists in Europe. The alliance between Catholicism and liberal democratic nationalism in Ireland, effected by O'Connell, was never an easy one, and there were always churchmen who were either opposed to or unhappy about the church's involvement with the nationalist movement. The reality was, of course, that many of the principles and social attitudes of English conservatism accorded closely with those of the Irish church, while the fundamental dispositions of liberalism and radicalism were substantially repugnant to it. It was the militant Protestantism of the Tories which rendered impossible what would have been the more natural alliance, and forced the church, in order to break the Protestant grip on Ireland, to treat with radicals and secularists who subscribed to propositions and principles condemned by the Papacy. The sectarian issue was, therefore, of the greatest importance in determining the politics of the church, but the outcome was something of a contradiction between the course dictated by tactics and that dictated by principle — and in consequence a very substantial weakening of the power and influence the church might have exerted had its principles and the pursuit of its social interests been in complete accord.

[1]   This is a central argument in my *Ireland's English Question*. For specific studies of this theme, see David W. Miller, *Church, State and Nation in Ireland 1898-1921* (Dublin, 1973); J. H. Whyte, *Church and State in Modern Ireland 1923-70* (Dublin, 1971). Other relevant studies are E. R. Norman, *The Catholic Church and Ireland in the Age of Rebellion 1859-1873* (London, 1965); P. Corish, 'Political Problems 1860-1878' in P. Corish (ed.) *A History of Irish Catholicism*, vol. 5, fascicule 3 (Dublin, 1967); J. H. Whyte, 'Political Problems, 1850-1860' in P. Corish (ed.) *A History of Irish Catholicism*, vol. 5, fascicule 2 (Dublin, 1967); E. Larkin, 'Church and State in Ireland in the Nineteenth Century', *Church History*. vol. xxxi, Sept., 1962.

English and Protestant observers took the prominence of the clergy in nationalist movements to prove that the clergy fostered and led such movements. Some clergy did, but to a very large extent the clergy were drawn into such movements in the wake of their flocks. Time and again, priests joined such movements for fear of losing all contact with, or control over, their people. And their purpose in joining was not to further nationalist agitation, but to suppress it so far as they could, at least within constitutional channels, and to preserve social morality. Those few priests who were extreme nationalist, such as was Father Patrick Lavelle in the 1860s, soon incurred ecclesiastical censure. All this made no impression on the English, nor did the fact that clerical influence was powerful only when it accorded with popular impulse. When, in 1883, and in 1888, Rome intervened with condemnations and instructions directed against the tactics of the Irish nationalist movement, these were not merely ignored, they were howled down by Irish populace and politicians for being what Protestants had always denounced—Roman and clerical intervention in Irish political affairs. On these occasions, English critics were indignant that the Irish had not obeyed their Roman ecclesiastical superiors, an obedience which on other occasions they deplored as slavish and depraved. And the whole history of secret societies in Ireland—constantly condemned by the clergy but constantly appearing and reappearing in considerable strength—also testifies to the refusal of many Irishmen to drop their political beliefs and principles at the clergy's command.

English blindness to these limitations on the church's power, and to the fact that many Irish nationalists regarded the church as an enemy, or at least a hindrance, to their objectives, sprang from the incomprehensions of prejudice. It is possible to dissect anti-Catholic prejudice in nineteenth-century Britain into component parts, but its real strength lay in its virtually instinctive nature and in its character as an immediate emotional response. Edmund Gosse's recollections of his childhood make this clear: '. . . I never doubted the turpitude of Rome. I do not think I had formed any idea of the character or pretensions or practices of the Catholic Church, or indeed of what it consisted, or its nature, but I regarded it with a vague terror as a wild beast, the only good point about it being that it was very old and was soon to die.'

Beyond this simple level of conditioned impulse ('You are a Catholic, sir!' cried the lady who saw A.W.N. Pugin cross himself in a railway compartment; 'Guard, let me out — I must get into another carriage!') the most basic source of anti-Catholicism was the widespread assumption that the Church of Rome had political claims subversive of the British constitution, a belief which Irish agitation was taken to confirm.[2]

This assumption, that Catholicism was a political danger, remains a continuing explanatory theme in English attitudes towards Ireland in the nineteenth century. Catholic emancipation, extorted in 1829 from a reluctant English government as a matter of expediency in the face of the threat of Irish disorder, was not an expression of genuine toleration, nor did it produce toleration. If anything, the measure heightened sectarian tension. This was not only because the English were antagonistic to the religious principles of Romanism as they understood it, but because of the way in which they had been compelled to concede ground — by mass popular turbulence, in which the priesthood was prominent. The Irish movement which produced Catholic emancipation confirmed the worst English fears of being confronted by priestcraft and popular Popery dedicated to destruction of the English constitution. Having been forced to give ground on the emancipation issue, English attitudes hardened against any further concessions to political Catholicism. O'Connell had erected an Irish national movement on a sectarian base. The result was to link Irish nationalism with Catholicism into a most powerful and effective political force. But it was also to confirm the sectarian hostility of the time so profoundly as

[2] A general account of Victorian anti-Catholicism is given by E.R. Norman, *Anti-Catholicism in Victorian England* (London, 1968), pp. 13-121. See also G.F.A. Best, 'Popular Protestantism in Victorian Britain' in R. Robson (ed.) *Ideas and Institutions of Victorian Britain*, (London, 1967), p. 115.

to nullify later attempts by Irish nationalists to bridge the sectarian chasm O'Connell's movement had opened up. In the long term, the cost of Catholic emancipation was to be partition.

The intensity of the English — and Irish Protestant — reaction to Catholic emancipation was related to a constitutional outlook which saw the arrangements of 1688 — the Protestant Constitution — as being final and sacred. The blow inflicted on the ancient Constitution in 1829 was followed by a second concentrated attack, this time from within Britain, the movement for parliamentary reform which produced the 1832 Act. At the same time, O'Connell was continuing to demand concessions towards Ireland, particularly in relation to tithes. One of his reactions to resistance was to suggest that Irish Catholics and English radicals come together in a democratic alliance, which might replace the House of Lords with an elective second chamber.

All this was too much for Tories, particularly Irish Tories, who took up sectarianism as a weapon to defend a constitution they saw as gravely imperilled: the 1830s and 40s were to see religious prejudice aroused and harnessed for political purposes as effectively as it was in the 1880s. Irish Protestant Tories began, in 1834, a campaign of public meetings and propaganda with the object of injecting the new British and Irish Protestant democracy with virulent no-Popery. The purpose was to defend the House of Lords, Protestant privilege, the landlord interest, the Union, and in general the constitutional *status quo* in church and state against what was depicted as a Popish conspiracy of subversion. The deliberate intention was to arouse prejudice and fear.

In the 1830s the cry of 'No Popery', related to Ireland, quickly aroused sentiments which were at the core of the British national experience since the Reformation. These old hatreds and fears were quickly given a contemporary framework. The story was circulated that O'Connell was in league with Popish priests, educated at the Roman seminary of Maynooth, where they were instructed in subversion of the British constitution, to be accomplished by repeal of the Union brought about through the violence of an ignorant peasantry. Such stores had sufficient factual pivots to give them wide credence, and they were often tied in with the terrors of Jacobinism and Chartism to increase their potential to arouse alarm.

In January 1848, the *Edinburgh Review* made a realistic appraisal of Tory tactics and of the destructive consequences of their campaign: 'Now that the Pope is powerless, and the Roman Catholic states do not dream of attacking the Protestantism of England, the Tory has taken up the discarded Whig principle of the last century and talks of the Protestant Succession, the Coronation Oath and the glorious Revolution of 1688 . . . Thus every generation runs a risk of being sacrificed to a sort of after-wisdom, and being governed by maxims which a former generation rightly adopted, but which are no longer applicable.'

Such judicious realism was, however, irrelevant to the popular mood which responded eagerly to the sectarian call. Whatever genuine religious animus was involved, the Tory campaign was a deliberate political contrivance in the interests of conservatism. As Professor Cahill has pointed out:

'. . . Conservatism derived much of its appeal from the fact that Conservatives linked their party ideology with British nationalism. Because of the close relationship between Protestantism and British nationalism, Conservative leaders, by treating the Irish Question as a religious one, could capitalize upon the emotional complex which influenced the public mind. By their manner of presenting the Irish Question, they directed the patriotic sentiments and feelings of the nation in favour of the Conservatives and against the Whigs, Liberals and Radicals . . . The fact that a No-Popery campaign based upon the Irish issue helped to unite the various interests within the Conservative party cannot be over-emphasized if the emotional force of conservatism as an ideology is to be understood'.

Very similar tactics were followed by Irish Unionists

between 1867 and 1886, as responses to the extensions of the franchise in 1867 and 1884, with similar efforts to mobilize British opinion against change and the threat of change in Ireland. 'No Popery' had great advantages as a tactic. Not only did it draw on emotions central to the national tradition, it also united Anglicans and Dissenters, and undermined the support of liberalism and radicalism. The newly emergent forces which pressed for change in Britain had strong connections with Dissent. But Dissent was very sensitive to the menace of Catholicism. The Irish question, presented as a religious one, could be used to weaken and divide these forces moving for parliamentary and social change. Not only might the fear of Popery divide the forces of reform, but they might also be saddled with a reputation for compromise with Popery and for weakness in regard to preservation of the national traditions. The deeply political and tactical nature of Tory sectarianism is obvious from the fact that they tried to shed the No-Popery mantle when it seemed to their political advantage to do so. Such was the case in the general election of 1859 when they attempted, with a remarkable degree of success, to attract the Irish Catholic vote.

But there was much more to anti-Catholic prejudice than concern, real — or feigned for political purposes — about its alleged threat to the British constitution. The priesthood and the sacramental system were held to be unmanly, un-English and unnatural. Particular objection was taken to the celibacy of the clergy, reckoned by Wordsworth in 1840 'the monstrous root of the greatest part of the mischief of Popery . . .', and a substantial English literature was devoted to the alleged sexual immorality and perversion associated with the priesthood and convents. As to the sacraments, Lord Salisbury was not prepared to accept confession as merely a religious matter: 'It so happens that this practice is deeply opposed to the peculiarities and idiosyncracies which have developed among the English people ever since they became a free people.'

This revulsion from Popery, its priests and practices, as being 'un-English' was reinforced by the fact that the revival of the Catholic Church in England from the 1830s took a particularly European form. This was not only so in terms of an ecclesiastical and doctrinal orientation towards the ultra-montane Papacy. Devotional life and religious practice were heavily influenced by French and Italian fashions. All this was made evident publicly in pronouncements and processionals, in spectacular conversions and no less spectacular triumphalist claims. To most of Protestant England, the 'foreign' and aggressively revived character of Catholic belief and ministry came as an affront and as a threat, particularly to those evangelical Protestants most intolerant of ritual and the claims and pretentions of Rome.

In contrast to the relatively quiet acceptance by the English public of Catholic emancipation, the government's intention to make a grant in 1845 to assist St Patrick's College at Maynooth with the training of the Irish priesthood led to a tremendous controversy. In 1829, as in 1845, Popery had been held to be repugnant to truth and morality, and dangerous to personal and national liberty, but whereas in the 1820s it seemed that emancipation must be conceded, no such mood prevailed in the 1840s in regard to further concessions. While emancipation could be stomached as unavoidable recognition of the unpalatable fact that Catholics existed, the 1845 Bill, and thereafter the whole matter of Irish claims for Catholic denominational education, raised the question of whether this reprehensible and erroneous religion, a menace to souls and society, should be allowed to perpetuate and extend itself by those who knew its true character. To support any form of Catholic education was to subsidize error, indeed worse, in the case of Maynooth, for it was popularly believed to be the centre of a conspiracy to subvert the constitution and overthrow property. Yet, in the storm of protest called forth by Sir Robert Peel's Maynooth Bill it was only his tactics that were really at issue. His intentions were orthodox enough. Assuming that priests were at the centre of Irish agitation, and that this was because they were beholden to the peasantry for their livelihood, he believed that financing Maynooth would make them less inclined to rely on the peasantry and more inclined to support the government's policies.

English unwillingness to support Catholic education was clearly related to a highly unfavourable estimate of the Catholic religion, and to the belief—which exists to this day, especially in Northern Ireland—that Catholic education was socially divisive. Although English governments were to stand firm against Catholic claims for separate education at the tertiary level until 1908, the theoretically non-denominational primary school system had long been converted in practice, since the 1850s, into a segregated one. Particularly in these circumstances, the protracted life of the Catholic education issue, in regard to university education became a continuing focus for sectarian animus. The English refusal to admit Catholic claims in education was taken to be not only an insulting and offensive estimate of Irish religious beliefs, but a denial of liberty of conscience, and indeed an active persecution. There could be no mistaking that English administrators envisaged education as a means of social control. This, as a generalized and positive attitude, was apparent early in the nineteenth century in the Whig belief that education was a cure-all for social ills and the basis of all true progress, a disposition expressed towards Ireland in the national education system begun in 1831. But this view of education also took the more specific form of regarding education as an instrument which could be used to eventually pacify Ireland, and to bring the Irish into line with English values and culture, while purging what was Irish.

It was this English approach, in which education became an aspect of political policy, which aroused the opposition of Irish nationalists, an opposition expressed at its most passionate in Pearse's characterization of the English education system in Ireland as 'The Murder Machine' deliberately designed to kill what was Irish. This English approach also aroused the deep antagonism of the Catholic church because obviously, 'sectarian' education could not be expected to produce what the English wanted and must in consequence be resisted. Conflict on this issue not only sustained nationalist animus and sectarian hostility, it gravely retarded educational development in Ireland, particularly that beyond the primary level. The socio-economic consequences of this were very considerable, hindering the growth of an Irish bourgeoisie and of a better educated society generally, and slowing the whole process of modernization. And, it could be argued, tradition, myth, and propagandist simplicities, remained major formative forces in Irish culture because the weakness of the areas of formal education left so much room for the informal environmental influences to operate. There can be no doubt of the remarkable influence of the national school system in diffusing an English culture in the nineteenth century. Although its Anglicizing tendencies were as much a response to a general cultural drift within Ireland as an active fostering of that process, it is tempting to speculate on what might have occurred to Irish culture had higher educational opportunity been more accessible. The national schools of which Pearse so vehemently complained as agencies of Anglicization were more than nine-tenths exclusively Catholic. Had Catholic higher educational claims been met when they were first pressed in the 1840s there is no reason to suppose that their cultural orientation would have been any less predominantly English. English religious prejudice prevented those claims being entertained. Had they been conceded, the history of Irish nationalism and of Anglo-Irish relations, might have been very different indeed.

Some of the reasons why this prejudice revived sharply from the 1830s have been outlined already. Another factor was the rapid growth of Irish immigration into Britain from about this time. What was apparent to the eye—increased numbers of Irish Papists—was interpreted for the ear by a concurrent invasion of virulently Protestant Irish orators who preached the menace of Popery up and down the country. The rationale of this crusade was the Irish Protestant belief that, as Catholic emancipation had put in some jeopardy the position of the Protestant ascendancy, it was necessary to make the British more aware of the evils of Popery so that no further concessions would be made to it. The siege mentality of Protestant Ireland at this time, and its feeling that it was being betrayed by British governments, is apparent in J. A. Froude's description of Irish evangelicalism as he found it in 1840:

'Their position was dangerous, and they knew it. They had nothing to hope for from the Government. Each year, in deference to the Catholic vote, their privileges were cut short, and their endowments diminished. But their spirit rose with their difficulties . . . and Protestantism was recovering the tone which two centuries before had overturned thrones and dynasties and shaken Romanism to its foundations.'

Some of these energies were invested in missions to convert the Irish peasantry, or in the dissemination of millions of Protestant tracts: such proselytizing became a continuing stimulus to sectarian conflict. Other of this energy was expended within Ulster in surges of revivalism, of which that of 1859 was the most significant. Central figures in all this, from the 1820s to the 1880s were first the Rev Henry Cooke, and then the Rev Hugh Hanna, whose ultra-Protestantism was vigorously anti-Catholic, pro-Unionist, and increasingly political in its practical application. Cooke and Hanna provided models for the Rev Ian Paisley, who is in their tradition of religious extremism and intransigence pursued by demagoguery.

Much of this renewed Protestant vigour was directed towards Britain, with the idea of stirring up such popular anti-Catholicism as would prevent or inhibit any further legislative concessions to Catholic Ireland. From the 1830s, the strongest elements in Irish Protestantism were endeavouring to use the prejudices of the British public against what was believed to be the pro-Catholic inclinations of the politicians.

Irish Protestant insistence on the menace of Catholicism found ready acceptance in the England of the Catholic revival. That revival's sanguine and eventually triumphalist tone gave countenance to claims that here again was the old enemy, Papal aggression, backed by a swelling Irish proletariat. The Protestant argument was supported by the fact that many Catholic clergy saw, in the Irish immigration, evidence of a divine plan to recover England for the true faith. In 1851 Archbishop MacHale of Tuam alarmed and enraged English Protestants by declaring that Irish immigration into England was 'sure to be as steady as the cruelty that continues to propel it will be untiring, until at length you [English] hear the exiled Catholics of Ireland addressing you from every quarter of England, in the language of Tertullian — We have filled your cities, towns, fields, armies, senate; the conventicles alone we leave to yourselves'.

This growing Irish occupation, inescapable to English eyes, was accompanied by striking public evidence of religious vigour — more priests, large new churches. Among the Irish in Britain the power of the priesthood was very great, in the Protestant estimate a sinister development. So was that alarming and disordered paradox which Froude had observed in Ireland in 1841: 'In Catholic Ireland at that time nothing seemed to be thriving except the Church. The poor creatures, while they starved themselves in hovels, were building everywhere massive chapels and cathedrals'. The same thing was happening in England. And, as Engels among others noted, the Irish attended these churches and practised their deplorable religion to an extent far greater than any other section of the working class.

These things were very worrying to those who did not comprehend them, or who were instinctively hostile. Here, mushrooming in Britain itself, was the Irish problem in microcosm — poverty, priestcraft, church wealth, potential unrest, and danger to the English state and religion. Few Protestants had any idea that the monolithic menace they saw growing in their midst was in fact afflicted by internal divisions and tensions between the old and the new, between what was English and what was Irish. The Englishman's image of Catholicism omitted this most basic flaw in its local strength and structures, and in consequence greatly exaggerated Catholic power and influence. This error prompted unwarranted fears and intransigence, to the worsening of Anglo-Irish relations. The reality is therefore worth investigating, particularly as this allows analysis of an aspect of Anglo-Irish relations from which the element of Catholic versus Protestant was removed and religion was a factor in common.

Since the Reformation, English Catholicism — almost entirely a religion of the upper classes — had schooled itself in the prudent ways of quietude. It shared many of the decorous religious attitudes and conservative social outlook of Anglicanism. To English Catholics the arrival of hordes of Irish co-religionists was a profoundly disturbing and unwelcome experience, whose religious responsibilities — to tolerate and assist — were accepted not without great difficulty and friction. At a dinner party given by the Marquis of Westminster, an English Catholic guest declared that she was 'an English Catholic not an Irish one, which is all the difference in the world. English Catholics are responsible human beings who are taught right from wrong, whereas Irish Catholics, belonging to a yet savage nation, know no better and are perhaps excusable on that account'. There was not only a social and cultural gulf. There was also a political one. English Catholic families were invariably conservative and usually strongly Unionist. Earlier in the nineteenth century, they were hostile to O'Connell's vigorous interventions in British politics, later they were just as antagonistic to Home Rule: the Duke of Norfolk and other leading English Catholics were prominent in defending the Union and condemning Irish agitation. English Catholic determination to prove Catholic loyalty by repudiating Irish causes was again evident in the Anglo-Irish war of 1920-21. All this aroused great indignation and intense hostility among the Irish generally. Protestants supposed automatically that a common religion united English and Irish Catholics. It did, within the sphere of religion — though even there internal disputes between English clerics and the Irish were frequent and bitter. And the same occurred in Scotland. But outside basic matters of religious belief, in the realm of politics and social life, the attitudes of English and Irish Catholicism were either worlds apart or at loggerheads. There was no basis whatever for Protestant fears of an Irish-English Catholic alliance.

For their part the Irish were not prepared to concede that English or Scottish Catholicism had any—let alone equal—spiritual value. To quote an Irish Catholic estimate made in Scotland, it was 'indifferent and decrepit . . . the degraded, the wretched and ignorant remnant of Catholicity . . .' This image was confirmed by the political behaviour of English Catholics, particularly in relation to the attempts of the English government to obtain Papal support for its Irish policies. English diplomacy at the Vatican became most active in the 1880s, through the agency of English Catholics in Rome, both clerical and lay. This produced some Papal action against the nationalist movement, action which was largely ineffective, not least because it could be held by the Irish to be English-inspired. This also showed, as the Irish saw it, just how degraded English Catholicism was, when it was prepared to assist the government in its efforts to mislead and pervert the Papacy, over which the Irish believed they had special claims springing from their long and stalwart loyalty to Rome in the face of persecution.

The result of this contemptuous opinion of English Catholicism was that its existence in no way qualified the image of England seen from across the Irish Sea. Indeed it confirmed it: even Catholicism had been corrupted by England. Nor does the fact that there was a rapidly growing Irish Catholic community in Britain seeem to have intruded in mitigation of that hostile estimate. Again, even the existence of Irish Catholics in Britain was turned to prove British depravity. The massive Irish 'leakage' from Catholicism in Britain was well beyond control even as early as 1840. Seen from Ireland, this was taken to be a very simple process: the Irish went to industrial Britain, many lost their faith and no longer practised their religion, therefore industrial Britain was to blame and was an evil, destructive environment. In fact, the phenomenon of loss of religious faith and practice among workers was general to the Industrial Revolution and urbanization. In so far as this was attributable among the Irish to want of churches and priests, the danger was simply not seen, and certainly not confronted, before irreparable damage was done—and if there was any neglect or blame in this, the Irish church was no less at fault than any other cause.

The fact that the Irish image of Britain was that of the destroyer of souls, despite the existence there of Catholicism, both English and Irish, points to the extraordinarily close—indeed inextricable—mingling of nationalism and religion in the Irish outlook. Irish attitudes towards England conformed so rigidly to a stereotype in which Gaelic Catholics confronted Protestant English that it was impossible to make room for Catholicism as an aspect of the English image: it was as if Ireland had a monopoly on Catholicism and examples of it elsewhere were but inferior imitations.

Irish folk tradition, preserving a sense of separateness, blended Irishness and Catholicism into a kind of mystical millennialism which was both anti-English and anti-Protestant. This blend was further hardened by the remarkable revival of the Catholic church in Ireland which followed the arrival of Archbishop—later Cardinal—Paul Cullen in Ireland in 1850. His reorganization and revitalization of the Church gave new vigour and power to the religious aspect of Irish life. That aspect, already central to the Irish sense of separate identity, became stronger and more aggressive and transmuted into what amounted to being the spiritual dimension of nationalism. That nationalism was seen to be dependent on the Catholic religion which gave rise to 'the purity of life which alone has saved our race from extinction'. This in turn meant that, because of its spiritual dimension, Irish nationalism and Ireland itself were superior to anything in England. England was a spiritually barren and heretical land, dedicated to wealth.

The conviction that Ireland was a 'spiritual nation', to use Pearse's term, was shared by both Irish nationalists and Irish religionists, though they meant somewhat different things by 'spiritual'. But in both cases they took this as proving their superiority to other peoples. In the nationalist version, this conviction of superiority tends to be implicit, while the explicit demand is simply for separation. However, in the Catholic version, the assertion of spiritual superiority is quite clear, as is the claim that Holy Ireland was chosen by God both to embody His teachings and to spread them abroad. There were many precedents for and repetitions of the claim made by Cardinal Logue in 1914 that Ireland was 'the most virtuous nation on the face of the earth' and many references to 'Ireland's spiritual Empire' abroad, and to the 'World-wide Empire of the Irish Race'. Here was indeed, to use the words of the Catholic liturgy 'a chosen race, a royal priesthood, a holy nation, a people set apart. Everywhere we proclaim your mighty works for you have called us out of darkness into your own wonderful light'.

How the Catholic Irish viewed the religious dimension of their relationship with England is nowhere better illustrated than in the words of the Irish Dominican preacher, Fr Tom Burke. 'Take an average Irishman,' said Burke in 1872, '. . . and you will find that the very first principle in his mind is, "I am not an Englishman, because I am a Catholic".' Burke argued that for centuries England had been trying 'to so mix up Ireland and England together that the Irish would lose sight of that past national history.' He then depicted this endeavour as presenting a choice between God and Mammon, between the spiritual and the material:

'But you may ask me, "Wouldn't it be better for Ireland to be as Scotland is—a prosperous and a contented province—rather than a distressed and a discontented nationality?" Which of these two would you have the old land to be, my Irish fellow-countrymen? To which of these two would you prefer to belong? to Ireland as a prosperous and a contented province, forgetful of her glorious national history, deprived of her religion, no light upon her altars, no God in the sanctuary, no sacramental hand to be lifted over the sinner's head—Ireland banishing the name of

Mary — Ireland canny and cunning, fruitful and rich, but having forsaken her God — Ireland blaspheming Patrick's name, Patrick's religion — turning away from her graves and saying: "There is no hope any more — no hope, no prayer;" but rich — canny, cunning and common-place . . . Ireland a province! No; rather be the child of a nation, rather be the son of a nation, even though upon my mother's brows I see a crown of thorns and on her hands the time-worn chains of slavery. Yet upon that Mother's face I see the light of faith, of purity, and of God; and far dearer to me is my mother Ireland, a nation in her sorrow today, than if I beheld her rich, and commonplace, and vulgar, and impure, and forgetful of herself and of God.'

Burke, and the many like him, had resolved the problems of Anglo-Irish relations down to a conflict between the service of God and of honour, and the service of wealth and vulgar worldliness. His definition of Irish nationality excluded anything not Catholic and everything English: it banished not only the Protestant but the Anglo-Irish. And it sought to give Ireland's attitude to the relationship with England the aspect of a crusade against the infidel and the heretic. On the other hand, Irish Protestants had cast the problems of the relationship into a form no less exclusive — the maintainence of a *status quo* which excluded Irish Catholics from positions of power and influence and which refused to recognize their claims to separateness as legitimate. Their attitudes were no less crusading for their essential defensiveness: they were defending the city of God against the onslaughts of the forces of Anti-Christ.

This raises, of course, the question of whether religion was a real and sincerely held dividing factor, or merely a badge of difference. There can be little doubt that it was both. The difference between Protestants and Catholics within Ireland, and between Catholic Ireland and Pro- testant England, was a real difference in that conflicting standpoints on religious fundamentals were at issue. However, this religious difference also entailed difference in values and world view and historical experience, and it was also a polarity which coincided with other differences — political, social, and economic — and indeed a focus around which these other differences grouped. In both of these opposed amalgams, religion was an inextricable element.

But what was most politically destructive about the religious conflict was not so much what was really involved, but the defective, false, and contemptuous image each religion had of the other. William Bulfin put the Catholic nationalist view:

'Broadly speaking, the Catholicism of Ireland is associated with Nationalism, simply because Catholicism is the religion of the majority of the Irish people, who in one form or another hold Nationalist opinions. The non-Catholics of Ireland, to a large extent, are un-Irish either in antecedents or sympathy. They are mostly Unionists in politics, not merely because of their religion, but because of their pockets. Unionism is largely a question of business. Thus the politico-religious war is a struggle between people who regard Ireland as their country and people who look upon it as the spoil of conquest . . . The cry of "No Popery" is simply a shibboleth on the lips of a party that follows the bread basket.'

However arguable its partial truth, this was too cynical and biased an estimate by far. It ignored the triumphalist aggressive face Catholicism presented to Protestants in Ireland. It bluntly denied the genuineness of Protestant belief in its anti-Catholic aspect. It implied that the Protestant religion was a sham and asserted that Protestants were 'un-Irish'. As a judgement, all this was distorted, offensive, or untrue: as a basis for political attitudes or action it was disastrous, for it was an expression of alienation and enmity which could only strengthen what it attacked.

The reverse also held. To Protestants, Catholicism — that amalgam of lies, ignorance, and superstition — was simply the ideology of sedition and tyranny, a front for the forces of violent republicanism. Home Rule was merely a cloak for the dispossession of Protestants as well as for Home Rule: 'There is not a Roman Catholic in Ulster to whom the promise of Home Rule does not mean the promise of the recovery of forfeited lands.' Like so many of the English images of Ireland, the English image of Irish Catholicism held an internal contradiction, but both elements were to that religion's denigration. One element was that wherein Irish Catholicism was obsessively depicted as Roman, not Irish, and therefore foreign: it was a sinister and dangerous intrusion of an external power into Ireland's affairs, an image which drew heavily on the central traditions of anti-Popery. But there was another element, one which went back before the Reformation to the period of the first conflicts between the two countries, in the twelfth century. This took the view that the Irish were not Catholics at all, nor even Christians: it was an image which grew out of the English need to find moral justification for their conquest by rejecting any Irish claims to civilization, of which the Christian religion was a central feature. It was impossible to deny that in Europe, Catholicism had produced a civilization to which, indeed, England was one of the heirs. So it must be supposed that the Irish, whatever they said, were only nominally Christian, and were really heathens and barbarians professing to be what their behaviour showed they were not. This denial of Irish Christianity, evident in the earliest English accounts of Ireland, reached its most intense in the sixteenth and seventeenth centuries, when it became ingrained in the national tradition, to survive well into the nineteenth century, if not, perhaps, into the twentieth. Irish Catholicism was not a religion at all, but a perversion and a sham. It was a vehicle for subversive politics, violence, ignorance, unprincipled morality, and material greed.

Given this estimate of Catholicism, there is much to support the analysis of the Protestant Irish parliamentarian Stephen Gwynn, made in 1907:

'England is always ready to credit evil of Ireland, partly because the long racial strife, in which Ireland has been the sufferer, has engendered dislike, for as the wise Roman said, it is a trait of human nature to hate those whom you have injured; and partly because it has been comfortable to saddle all the misery of Ireland upon the imputed defects of Irish character. But, above and before all, England has always readily believed the worst of Ireland, and distrusted Ireland because of that ingrained and inbred detestation of Catholicism which is to be found in almost every Englishman. There is the true root of the Irish difficulty. The ascendancy party in Ireland have always been able to appeal to this prejudice, and have never appealed in vain. The result has been to breed in Protestant Ireland a feeling towards Catholics like that of the ruling race in countries where there is a colour bar.'

It is, of course, a fact that the blatantly un-Christian attitudes and behaviour of some of those acting in the name of religion have caused some observers to dismiss the reality or genuineness of religious motivation; they forget Acton's aphorism: 'Fanaticism in religion is an alliance of the passions she condemns with the dogmas she professes.' And they forget how deep are the socio-cultural ties which still link those whose practice of religion has long since fallen away, or never existed, with the traditional religious divisions and their standpoints. The religious fanaticism characteristic of earlier centuries is still operative in Anglo-Irish relations, and within Ireland, not only as such, but also in the form of a residue of suspicions, hostilities, and prejudices it has bequeathed to those of genuine religious beliefs, and even more importantly, to those who profess none. Probably the most destructive aspect of the religious situation was the image each religion made for itself of the other. It amounted to a denial of the reality of that religion as a religion. This had the paradoxical effect of leading both religions to seriously underestimate each other's genuine power and tenacity, while at the same time grossly exaggerating each other's potential menace. In both cases, the face of the other religion was seen as a thin mask for the political aggressor beneath. The outcome was a long history of insults and contempt, hatred and fear, mistakes, blunders and neglects, which continues still. What was, and is, in conflict, was not two religions, but two distorted and defective images of religion.

7

Violence and Counter-Violence

IF the issue of religion is at the centre of the history of Anglo-Irish relations, so is the matter of violence. And just as a curious discord existed in the English image of Irish religion — Roman and Irish — so it did in the English understanding of violence in Ireland. In vindicating the morality of conquest and maintaining the image of the Irish as uncivilized, it was important for the English to claim that the Irish were incurably violent. The idea that the Irish were naturally violent became part of British historical tradition, not only because it justified English rule, but because it explained why it had been so constantly challenged: the fault lay not in English rule but in the refusal or inability of the Irish to turn from their barbarous ways. In their predeliction for violence, the Irish placed themselves at odds with normal human values accepted everywhere else. An English estimate of 1610 had it that 'That which is hateful to all the world besides, is only beloved and embraced by the Irish. I mean civil warres and domesticall discentions'. The image of violence as being a national characteristic of the Irish still survives.

Were the truth or otherwise of this to be investigated, it would require an evaluation of the extent to which Irish violence was a response to English violence in Ireland, as well as analysis of the question of whether English treatment based on the supposition that the Irish were violent, actually created what was supposed to exist already. In 1909, Bishop Henry W. Cleary published *An Impeached Nation being A Study of Irish Outrages*. This long and detailed study set out to prove that the Irish were 'the least crimeful nation in the British Isles, and one of the most moral, clean-living, polite and naturally law-abiding peoples on the face of the planet'. Cleary's argument was not only that the Irish had been provoked by oppression and terrorism far greater in its violence than any with which they had responded, but that reports of Irish outrages and crime had been consistently invented and exaggerated for political purposes. He contended that the 'Irish Orange-Tory ascendancy party' manufactured and magnified stories of Irish violence in order to alarm the English parliament and people, thus creating a climate favouring repression, against reform or Home Rule, and in general supporting maintenance of ascendancy policies and dominance. Cleary's was the most extensive development of an argument frequently advanced by Irish nationalists, and his case, asserting various kinds of misrepresentation of the Irish crime situation, was well documented. The English, however, were at no time interested in such defences: Cleary, and other Irishmen who argued a similar case, preached only to the converted. The presumption of innate and excessive Irish violence was too useful politically to be queried. Besides, by the time of Cleary's book, the Irish reputation for barbarous and gratuitous violence had been established in English minds for centuries. This Irish violence did more than justify conquest and rule. It justified English violence. The basic morality supporting English violence in Ireland was the claim that it was necessary in order to suppress Irish violence. The history of Irish rebellions made it apparent that it was always the Irish who initiated violence. The English paid no attention at all, until very recent years, to the possibility that their rule might embody what is now called institutionalized or established violence, that is, governmental, administrative, and legal structures which bore down coercively on individuals and social groups. English government in Ireland was assumed to be potentially excellent, if only the Irish did not persist in frustrating it and compelling it to act against them.

The image of the Irish as an entire people wedded to violence was, however, not a tenable one for use in practical politics. Necessity—and hope—dictated another image, which qualified substantially the totality of the first:

'. . . there are two Irelands—the Ireland of men of all parties, and creeds, and ranks, and callings, who, whatever else they differ upon, unite in wishing to preserve law and order and the right of every citizen to go about his business in peace and safety; and there is the other Ireland—the smaller Ireland, as I firmly believe—of the men who foment and condone and sympathize with crime.'

This pronouncement, by G. O. Trevelyan, Irish Chief Secretary in 1883, set out a division necessary to the principles of English Liberals and to the practical policies of all English governments. In Tudor times, and later, it was convenient and acceptable to see English rule as being resisted by the Irish, *en masse*. As the nineteenth century progressed, this depiction became less and less tolerable because it cast the English as rulers of a people against the will of the majority, and thus in the role of oppressors. It therefore became common to locate resistance to English rule among an Irish minority and to claim that the majority opposed such criminals and were really supporters of all that English rule stood for. By this device of claiming that there were two Irelands, of which that opposed to England was by far the smaller, it was possible to defend and justify the ethics of English rule and of consequent policies. It was a contention which seemed to be supported by fact, for those Irishmen who were prepared to go to the extreme of resorting to violence were always a tiny minority. The English habit, as it developed in the later nineteenth century, of setting up a sharp division—indeed an opposition—between the men of peace and the men of violence had the effect of isolating, in English minds, the men of violence from the real, majority, Ireland, and of elevating violence and those who used it, into the entirety of the Irish problem. The tendency was to regard those who used violence, not as extremists in the sense of representing the extreme development of attitudes which existed in less extreme forms in the whole Irish community, but as separate, apart from, that community.

This interpretation was fostered by the tendency of Irish

violence to be associated with a succession of secret societies, whose small size, and condemnation by the Catholic Church, suggested to English authorities that they were an aberration in Irish society. These societies were, in fact, a normal and permanent feature of Irish life whose continuing existence pointed to an enduring anti-English disaffection. Some few Englishmen could see this. Augustine Birrell told the Royal Commission on the 1916 Rebellion: 'The spirit of what today is called Sinn Feinism is mainly composed of the old hatred and distrust of the British connection, always noticeable in all classes, and in all places, varying in degree, and finding different ways of expression, but always there as the background of Irish politics and character.' Most Englishmen found this unacceptable: they preferred to regard themselves as hated by the abnormal few, rather than by the many. English governments tended to miss the basic lesson of Irish violence, that it was an extreme manifestation of a widespread, if sometimes buried, national mood, and not an isolated or merely criminal aberration.

This image of Irish violence, necessary for English ethics and peace of mind, was also a political necessity. Only by assuming that the violence was located among a few, and in no way a reflection of the real mood of Ireland, could the Irish situation be envisaged as controllable. Irish violence was seen as a kind of self-contained disease, to be stamped out within its own confines, rather than a symptom indicative of disorders in the whole body politic. This view was characteristic of the English coercionist tradition generally, which was based on the assumption that strong measures would solve the problem of Irish unrest, and was particularly notable in military circles. 'The vital point is to deal with the Thugs . . .' insisted Sir Hamar Greenwood to the British cabinet in May 1920, a conviction Greenwood linked — in a juxtaposition typical of this mentality — with the opinion that crime and violence were rife because of the inadequacy and weakness of the civil government. The idea that once the terrorists — the 'gunmen', 'the men of violence' — were caught, then the problem was solved and all would be well, re-emerged after 1968 in the political stock-in-trade of Northern Ireland Unionists. It was a necessary belief in that it located the trouble outside Unionist policies in a small criminal minority which could be destroyed by superior force and without major policy changes by the ruling party. Whatever progress was made towards destruction or apprehension of 'the men of violence' could be depicted as movement towards a real solution. All this, and the claims made for the effectiveness of the British Army after 1969, had precedents in 1920-21. Then, there was also the tendency of the law enforcement forces to give glowing accounts of their success, and to engage in recurrent predictions of the impending immediate demise of the Irish Republican Army.

The fact that, in 1921, though the English did not know it, the IRA's limit of endurance was fast approaching was of military importance, but it was relevant to a full settlement of Irish affairs only if the IRA itself was the entirety of the problem. Even if this was so — which, given the dimensions of Irish politics and public opinion, was too narrow a view to be tenable — the problems remained of how to eradicate or neutralize entirely a guerilla force, and how to banish fear. The military interpretation of how to solve the Irish question was deficient within its own limitations for it had little bearing on the fact that it was not only actual violence and terror which had dominated the crisis points of Irish history, but, much more pervasively, widespread fear of violence and terror. Intimidation has long been a tactic used by Irish extremists. It was part of the world of Carleton's peasantry just as it is part of contemporary Belfast. Nor does such intimidation need to be overt, or directed against every individual to ensure its success. Many of those 60,000 Belfast people — 12 per cent of the population of the city — whom the Community Relations Commission reports to have been intimidated and forced to leave their homes between 1969 and 1972, would have done so, not under direct compulsion, but in fearful anticipation of it. A relatively low level of actual violence, or indeed none at all, can sustain a high level of fear and induce behaviour desired by extremists and destructive of social order and stability. This phenomenon was just as remarkable in nineteenth-century rural Ireland as in Northern Ireland since 1968. It is possible to reduce drastically the incidence of overt violence or instances of direct intimidation without any corresponding progress towards settlement of the situation. Military activity directed against 'the men of violence' cannot destroy, at least in any way quickly, the fear generated by their violent image, and thus it cannot liberate a community from attitudes and behaviour related to the expectation of violence.

Nor can it lay ghosts. If anything, it adds to their number, to judge from an Irish political martyrology to which names are still being added. In his 1915 pamphlet, 'Ghosts', Pearse raised 'ghosts of dead men that have bequeathed a trust to us living men . . . The ghosts of a nation sometimes ask very big things; and they must be appeased, whatever the cost'. According to Pearse, these ghosts—of Tone, Davis, Lalor, Mitchel, and Parnell —asked Irishmen to take up and serve the cause of separation of Ireland from England. He quoted Mitchel: 'In the case of Ireland now there is but *one fact* to deal with, and *one question* to be considered. The fact is this—that there are at present in occupation of our country some 40,000 armed men, in the livery and service of England; and the *question* is—how best and soonest to kill and capture those 40,000 men.'

As to the cost of achieving separation, Pearse did not regret it, he exulted in it: '. . . bloodshed is a cleansing and a sanctifying thing, and the nation which regards it as the final horror has lost its manhood. There are many things more horrible than bloodshed; and slavery is one of them'.[1] Pearse mustered his ghosts to testify to this conclusion, and the outcome was the 1916 rebellion which added more, and

---

[1] For recent critiques of Pearse's attitude towards violence, see Francis Shaw, S. J., 'The Canon of Irish History—A Challenge', *Studies*, vol. lxi, no. 242, Summer, 1972, pp. 115-53; Cathal B. Daly, *Violence in Ireland* (Dublin, 1973).

more recent ghosts to those he invoked. The military arm of England was not equipped to overthrow 'the awful tyranny of the dead'.

There is much to support the argument that the forms and procedures of democracy are recent developments in Ireland and that violence and rebellion are much more central to the experience and traditions of the nation. On an overview of Irish history, it is hardly too much to say that violence, or incipient violence, was the normal condition in which society existed. This may be illustrated by an examination of rural disorder in the early decades of the nineteenth century, which suggests, on a comparison with other periods of overt violence—including that in contemporary Northern Ireland—that the pattern and features of violence, and its stimulus, have a general consistency over a long period of time.

In the years immediately following the Union, the British government in Ireland failed to concern itself with major peasant grievances—rents, tenancy, evictions, the tithe. The consequence was a degree of popular unrest, virtually leaderless, which issued in a widespread collapse of British rule. Particularly for periods between 1813 and 1823 much of the south and west of Ireland fell under the domination of peasant 'armies' from which landlords and magistrates fled. To see Irish violence in terms of the explicit challenges made by Irish nationalists to English rule—1798, 1848, 1867, 1916—is to gravely underestimate its extent, and to grossly overestimate the degree to which English rule, and English concepts of law and order, prevailed in Ireland. Throughout the nineteenth century, the nationalist rebellions represented a very minor aspect of Irish violence, however important to both sides might be the principles involved. At the same time as parts of rural Ireland effectively rejected English rule, sectarian clashes, especially in Ulster, were frequent, and usually quite uncontrolled; they were sometimes organized, as in 1815, when an information centre was established in Armagh to allow Catholics and Protestants to nominate fairs where they could meet to fight. These clashes, with their seventeenth and eighteenth-century roots, were channelled into growing industrialized Belfast, where they took new form in competition for jobs and in the rapid territorializing of the city into ethnic-religious areas. The elections of December 1833 established what was to become a familiar pattern — ferocious fighting in the streets, inability of political leaders to restrain followers, and loss of control by the police.

Even where English law and order formally prevailed, the real loyalty of the peasant was to his own traditional laws, and as Galen Broeker puts it, 'to what was in effect his own government — government in the form of the agrarian secret societies, whose political activity took the form of agrarian outrage'. In 1836, secret societies were described by Sir Cornewall Lewis as a 'vast trade union for the protection of the Irish peasantry'. That is, the Irish peasant looked not to the government, but to his own primitive resources and organization to preserve his way of life, by violence where necessary.

The government was unable to control this situation, let alone stamp it out. Its use of police generated hatred and resentment, for their numbers were usually inadequate in the face of mass demonstrations and their fear caused them to over-react brutally. As early as 1813 the use of the army in a police capacity had become accepted practice. Nor was the Catholic priesthood able to control violence and terror: priests were often terrorized themselves. The government tactic of employing informers and spies led to a poisoning of society and to barbarous vengeances. The government's tendency was to differentiate between Protestant and Catholic violence: both were condemned, but that of 'loyalists' was the more understandable and excusable. Some English officials even regarded the prospect of open rebellion with approval. This would clear the air, and bring the secret troublemakers into the open where they could be dealt with. In 1813 the Lord Lieutenant of Ireland, Lord Whitworth, observed to Peel that another revolution might be good for Ireland. There would be killing, but over-all 'the results would be favourable to the tranquillity of the country'. Given the confidence that England could cope easily with whatever rebellion Ireland might be able to stage, such violence was seen as a solvent for the difficulties of ordinary government.

Of special importance in destroying any basis for trust in dealing with England were the activities of the English 'secret service' in procuring informers and in acting as *agents provocateurs*, and the alleged willingness of the English government to resort to forgery, lies, and connivance in crime in order to frustrate and discredit Irish nationalism. The documented history of this activity goes back at least to the time of Pitt, and extends to the allegations of the Littlejohns in March 1974 that they had been employed by the British secret service to rob banks and engage in other criminal activity in order to discredit the IRA. Probably the most spectacular case of these tactics was the efforts of *The Times* in 1887 to link Parnell with the Phoenix Park murders of 1882, through the use of letters later proved to have been forged. Later evidence was to suggest the involvement of prominent English politicians of the day, notably A. J. Balfour and Lord Salisbury, in facilitating this: 'The evidence is there, the corruption is there, the shamelessness is there, the debauchery of the "public service" by the higher servants of the State is there: all for political ends against Ireland.'—such was Casement's judgement in viewing the documentation in 1914. Irish nationalist opinion held—and still holds—the English capable of any infamy, any departure from morality or principle, in their dealings with Ireland. This widespread Irish belief, that the English could be neither believed nor trusted, contributed much towards inducing less faith in talk, more in force.

The normalizing of violence in Ireland was a direct product of the English refusal to attend to Irish grievances unless they were expressed violently. In 1889, Lord Salisbury said as much. He believed that the great majority of Englishmen would never concede Home Rule to Ireland unless their political instincts suddenly changed, and that could be achieved only by violence: 'Nations do not change their political nature like that, except through blood. It would require a subordination of all ordinary motives, a renunciation of traditions and prepossessions, a far-reaching and disciplined resolve, which is never engendered by mere persuasions, but only comes after conflict and under the pressure of military force'.

The period 1916-21 was to prove this assessment accurate, but the comment was not so much a prediction, as the expression of a frame of political mind utterly impervious to being changed by argument. It invited the test of violence and doomed to irrelevance constitutional and parliamentary efforts to secure changes. As John Dillon told the House of Commons on 11 May 1916: 'You are letting loose a river of blood . . . between two races who . . . we had nearly succeeded in bringing together . . . you are washing out our whole life work in a sea of blood.'

This English attitude of mind compelled Irish nationalist leaders to adopt methods which, if they stopped short of direct violence, were necessarily forceful. 'The first thing you have to do with an Englishman on the Irish question is to shock him. Then you can reason with him right enough' — such was Joseph Biggar's justification for the Irish tactic of obstruction in the House of Commons in the early 1880s. Shocking the English was, however, a tactic of very limited efficacy, for if it aroused attention it also aroused hostility. England would attend only to violence in some form. But when violence took place English politicians argued that to make any substantial concession would be to bow to force, which would be morally intolerable and tactically wrong. To the Irish, failure to gain any or sufficient concessions indicated that the violence used had been insufficient to achieve the objective: the lesson was to use more. This standard pattern was followed after the 1916 rebellion. In June 1916 Walter Long and Lord Lansdowne attacked Lloyd George's proposals for a settlement, arguing that concession of Home Rule at that point would be a surrender to force, something bad in itself as well as inviting further pressure to extort more concessions. Yet it was also a fact, as it proved, that the refusal to make concessions also invited the continuance of pressure.

The normalizing of violence in Belfast, while influenced by these general factors, is something of a special case. In the early nineteenth century Belfast experienced rapid economic growth, attracting to it the surrounding rural population in such a way as to intensify to extremes the sectarian hostility already present in Ulster as a whole. This was because Belfast's growth was, at first, experienced as a Catholic invasion. Belfast in the mid-eighteenth century had a population only 6.5 per cent Catholic: by 1834 it was 31 per cent and by 1848, 43 per cent Catholic. This influx of Catholics aroused Protestant fears that they would be overwhelmed, and prompted the growth of a siege mentality expressed in public displays of Protestant supremacy and the determination to exclude Catholics from Protestant areas of living and employment. Catholics responded with their own demonstrations, usually associated with nationalist causes, such as that of Repeal in the 1840s. Clashes between sectarian mobs became common, territorial segregation became entrenched, and the 'normal' methods of Belfast violence became established —street warfare, house-wrecking, stone-throwing, and intimidation.[2] At least once in every decade in the nineteenth century, simmering disorder boiled over into major violence, so that in his recollections, published in 1917, John Morley could describe Belfast as harbouring a spirit of bigotry and violence for which a parallel could hardly be found in any town in Western Europe. The efforts of the government to repress this violence had short-term effect in particular eruptions, but no long-term pacificatory effect.

One reason for this was that any government intervention in sectarian conflict was itself construed as sectarian. Attempts to restrain Protestant bigotry were taken as showing that the Government was pro-Catholic and must be

[2] The most extensive coverage of the history of violence in Belfast is Andrew Boyd, *Holy War in Belfast* (Tralee, 1969).

See also Sybil E. Baker, 'Orange and Green. Belfast, 1832-1912', in Dyos and Wolff (ed.) *The Victorian City*, pp. 789-814.

resisted as such. Repression of Catholic violence proved what Catholics already knew, that the Government was merely another form of Protestant persecution. But only too often the instruments of law enforcement were used with marked partiality. The police were mainly Protestant and their sympathies predictable. In observing 'what amounted to civil war' in Belfast in August 1920, the English journalist Hugh Martin remarked that the British Army showed 'an extraordinary tenderness for the feelings of Orangemen, whom they seemed to regard as loyal, though possibly mistaken, friends, while Catholics were all simply, "Sinn Feiners", and, therefore, enemies . . . in only too many instances the Army was maintaining order by doing nothing while Catholic quarters were being sacked'.

There were other reasons why Belfast violence became entrenched. Its concentration, during the nineteenth century, in west Belfast, meant that it did not intrude on the homes or the lives of the middle class. Just as the population of England found violence in remote Ireland tolerable because they were not confronted with it personally, so the Protestant establishment in Belfast could readily endure what they seldom encountered, particularly when it could be seen to be protecting their interests. There were also reasons, concerned with the nature of the city, which favoured violence. The most obvious of these was poverty and insecurity. In housing, public amenities, education, social welfare, the provision for leisure activities, hygiene, law enforcement, even in the provision of police, Belfast was a case of gross neglect. Its industries were subject to economic fluctuations which produced un-employment, fierce competition for jobs, low wages, and insecurity — as well as sectarian discrimination. Here was a situation in which the pressures of urban industrialism were at their worst, breeding frustration and violence which fed on themselves and which attracted from the rest of Ireland both criminals and agitators. In all this, Belfast was hardly an exception among cities of the Industrial Revolution, except perhaps in degree. But there were other factors peculiar to the religious character and history of the city.

'Riots and revivals were the emotional release in an impoverished working-class culture where politics and religion were the only respectable activities'. The culture of the city had taken a divisive sectarian form. Churches and church organizations monopolized social life and recreations — with the exception of drinking, though even that was conducted mainly in segregated pubs. Throughout the nineteenth century, and thereafter, drunkenness and outbreaks of violence were closely associated. But a factor frequently overlooked is that violence provided an element of excitement, and drama, and a dimension for romance and heroism, in an environment otherwise harsh, drab, and stifling. In assessing Belfast as 'A Fighting City' in 1919, J. W. Good made much of the love of fighting for its own sake — encouraged, he contended, by those who sought to divide and rule, and given the aspect of barbarism by those who introduced large quantities of arms and ammunition. This last merely increased the excitement:

'When it became the fashion for half Belfast to go about its business and its pleasure with a revolver in its hip-pocket, life was more exciting than it is in Albania or in a mining town as shown in cinema films of the wild and woolly West. I have seen a drunken [Ulster] Volunteer reeling home on a Saturday night blaze furiously at a street lamp; and at hotly contested football matches a goal would be greeted by a salvo of revolver shots from the spectators, which sent mud and gravel spirting up almost under the feet of the players.'

No doubt the hooligan element and the thirst for simple if dangerous adventure were part of Belfast violence and, as Good claimed, there were times when the 'majority hugely enjoy their skirmishes', but hate and hysteria and fear became the dominant factors in the twentieth century as tendencies towards violence were organized and armed in relation to disciplined sectarian and political private armies.

In contrast with the more spectacular violence of Belfast, the normal violence of the nineteenth-century Irish countryside presents an even more repulsive picture, sordid in its cruel sameness in various times and places. In the

1850s Irish agrarian relations were at a level resembling guerilla warfare. Landlords and land agents carried arms as a matter of course: the peasants killed them when they could. In 1882 a force of a hundred armed men was thought necessary to undertake the seizure of cattle from one tenant in arrears: there were 3,432 agrarian outrages in that year alone. Belfast violence was between Irishmen, self-contained as it were, but in the rest of Ireland violence was directed against English rule and its adjuncts, particularly landlordism. It could well be argued that for almost the entirety of the nineteenth century Ireland was in a condition of incipient mass rebellion. Why did it not occur?

In 1843, Engels, assessing the Irish element in the British Isles declared: 'Give me two hundred thousand Irishmen and I could overthrow the entire British monarchy'. Here were 'Men who had nothing to lose . . . real proletarians and sansculottes' with enormous potential as rebels. But as Engels saw, Daniel O'Connell would not use 'his millions of militant and desperate Irishmen' for revolution: he was a bourgeois, frightened of the people, using them merely for his own political advancement.

Motivations aside, Engel's general conclusion was valid, not only in regard to O'Connell, but also to many subsequent popular leaders. They did not want violence. They were prepared to use the threat of violence to secure constitutional reforms, and their popular power and the extent of their progress towards reform enabled them to contain the primitive forces which made this progress possible. In the eyes of the English, O'Connell and Parnell, and lesser Irish leaders in the constitutional tradition, seemed a dreadful threat, and representative of Ireland at its worst. In fact their function was to repress that worst threat — violence — and to shield England from the 'natural' consequences of the situation in which the Irish peasant was imprisoned. Here one may turn to consider what Barrington Moore in *Social Origins of Dictatorship and Democracy* calls 'the costs of going without a revolution'. He contends:

'The assumption that gradual and piecemeal reform has

demonstrated its superiority over violent revolution as a way to advance human freedom is so pervasive that even to question such an assumption seems strange . . . [but] the costs of moderation have been at least as atrocious as those of revolution, perhaps a great deal more'.

Arguably, the cost of O'Connell's moderation, or of Parnell's harnessing the forces behind the Land War, was to protract, agonizingly, a relationship between England and Ireland which was painful and damaging to both. Perhaps here is support for Barrington Moore's thesis that the really sick societies are those in which revolutions are impossible. Certainly Irish no less than English politicians contrived to stifle a violence repugnant to them.

Violence and disorder were regarded as thoroughly bad by the English and by those Irishmen who accepted the English constitutional tradition. Both saw violence as indicative of Irish shortcomings, to the extent of agreeing that its prevalence was an argument against giving the Irish self-government. Violence was something to be ashamed of, and a grave political disability. The use of such criteria to appraise Irish affairs ignored England's own past, where revolutionary violence and civil war in the seventeenth century was integral to a historical process which made peaceful change possible thereafter. England had had its revolution, and learnt from it, and this was commonly held (at least in the classical Whig interpretation) to loom large among the reasons why the crises of the nineteenth century were weathered peacefully and why a stable condition of law and order prevailed.

Nor did the English consider the possibility that their government of Ireland could itself be experienced as violent. Admittedly it was coercive in its efforts to maintain law and order, but this was rendered necessary by the behaviour of the Irish: that they should be aggrieved at the inevitable consequences of their own actions was ridiculous. It was inconceivable that law and order should be regarded as repressive, or that English ideas about property and government, when given legislative form, should be seen as provocative, institutionalized violence. And it was not only

English conservatives who revered the English idea of law and order: it also took on the complexion of a romantic cause. In 1887 R. L. Stevenson, who was sympathetic to Home Rule, declared his intention of going to Ireland to live with a family who were being terrorized, so that he might be assassinated in defence of law and order.

Stevenson's reduction of the Land War to a 'cowardly business' was characteristic of the English belittlement of Irish violence: they would not take even that seriously. Later — and currently — the use of the labels 'gunman' and 'terrorist' for those whose self-image was that of 'patriot' was a similar attempt to equate nationalism with criminality and so destroy or diminish its claims to good reputation. These English efforts to give violence the image of degradation had little impact, for they were thwarted by an Irish imagery which tended to glorify and glamorize it. Besides, the more the English response was to dismiss the violence as futile, criminal, and the madness of the few, the more the Irish were determined to prove it was the reverse. And the louder the English denunciations, the more efficacious, the more wounding, the Irish took that violence to be. There was also the real problem of what else the Irish could do to seek changes they wanted. True, they could attempt to persuade parliament by the use of reason. But Salisbury had made clear that the English were impervious to argument, and in the late 1840s Macaulay testified that he, at least, was impervious to Irish hatred. Macaulay had wondered to himself why it was that Irish hatred of the English did not excite his hatred in return: 'I imagine that my national pride prevents it. England is so great that an Englishman cares little what others think of her, or how they talk of her.' Make the English care, then: the Irish, or at least some of them, did not need the declarations of men like Salisbury or Macaulay to teach them this. It seemed to them to be the whole lesson of Anglo-Irish history. And if further evidence was necessary to discredit English versions of law and order and to prove the efficacy of violence, it was offered by the confrontation between Ulster Unionists and the English government from 1910. It was then proved that resort to the threat of violence against the law and order of England could succeed.

That success was, however, no real model for Irish nationalism. It was a negative success, preventing something not wanted, a preservation of the *status quo* according with a substantial area of English opinion, and backed by remarkable unity of conviction and emotion. Nationalist Ireland wanted something new, whose extent was unclear, and for which support was uncertain and divided, and against the real inclinations of most Englishmen. Its achievement, to the extent that the Irish Free State of 1921 represented what nationalist Ireland wanted, was reached through violence. That violence was not merely the Irish violence which began in 1916: which would never have been sufficient to effect the transformation of English mind necessary to allow the requisite political change. Rather was it the fact that Irish violence took place in the context of the far more massive and psychologically disturbing violence of the First World War. It was this which ultimately changed all things utterly. But what is most remarkable about English attitudes towards violence in Ireland in the years 1920-1 is how little, not how much, they had changed.

As the Anglo-Irish war intensified, IRA terror being matched if not exceeded by that of the Black and Tans, it was reported as common in Ireland to believe that if the people of England were really aware of what was happening in Ireland, they would demand it be stopped. If this was so, it reflects an enhanced image of England, of a kind Dillon might have claimed as indication that the two peoples had come closer together. But it was an illusion. The people of England did know, and most them either did not care, cr believed that a tough Irish policy ('wipe 'em out' was the opinion of a third class railway compartment in England in November 1920) was entirely justified.[3] There was in fact

[3] Philip Gibbs maintained in 1921 that the English people were 'darkly ignorant' of what was happening in Ireland in regard to English brutality. (Preface to Hugh Martin, *Ireland in Insurrection* (London, 1921), pp. 11-12). But as Gibbs himself notes, this was not so much a lack of information, as that people in England regarded it as 'mere malignant rumours, or as wild Irish lies'. The situation was

no significant conflict between the government's Irish policy and English public opinion. In 1920, the government's conviction was that a policy of reprisals was necessary and salutary. The moral justification was quite simple: the forces of English law and order were the victims of a condition of terrorism which compelled them, in order to combat it effectively, to react in kind. This was a matter of specific tactics: the government took a no less vigorous line on the question of general strategy. As late as May 1921, Lloyd George argued in cabinet for a continuation of the war in Ireland, perhaps for another three years if necessary. He contended that it might be better to crush the Irish than engage in some immediate sentimental compromise which would make trouble for the future: he envisaged an Irish exploitation of any measure of independence to an extent so intolerable as eventually to compel Britain to reconquer Ireland.

The government's Irish policy did come under increasing criticism within Britain. Such criticism as emanated from the Labour Party or independent Liberals—the opposition —could be seen in the context of an attempt to make political capital, but no such charge could be laid against the most vigorous critics, a very small group of intellectuals and public figures, associated with the Peace With Ireland Council. Their position was that the government's policy was contrary to all traditions of British life and behaviour. It was no such thing. It was a continuation, and modernization, of punitive and coercive policies pursued throughout the nineteenth century. Nor was the fact that the consciences and principles of a minority were affronted by anything unprecedented: the treatment of Ireland had been the subject of English minority protest before. And the protestors of 1920-21, despite their public prominence, were still very much a minority—excluding, for instance, most of the churches,

similar to that claimed to prevail in the United Kingdom with regard to army and policy brutality in 1971—'No one wanted to know. Those who did know did not care' (Tony Smythe, Preface to *Northern Ireland. The Mailed Fist. A Record of Army & Police Brutality from Aug. 9-Nov. 9 1971.* Campaign for Social Justice in Northern Ireland (Antrim, 1971) p. 3.

the Catholic as well. A number of reasons may be proposed to explain why this minority protest took on such importance. There was the war weariness and revulsion from violence that followed the war. There was some faltering, among a few, of faith in the efficacy of British power. There was far more English awareness of what was happening in Ireland, a development associated with general improvements in communications and news coverage, and particularly with very effective Irish propaganda, not only in words but in spectacular deeds — such as Terence MacSwiney's fast to the death in Brixton prison.

But the most important reasons why minority criticism existed and why the government was influenced by it were quite other than these. Quite simply, the government's coercionist policy was not working, or so it appeared. For all that the military claimed progress, and for all that cabinet's preference was for a hard line — 'In dealing with the Irish you must show that you mean to go on', argued Lloyd George — continued coercion was not producing sufficient results fast enough. What it was producing was a rising tide of internal criticism, politically discomforting and damaging to the government. Gradually the government became aware that, however appropriate it seemed in theory, in practice the coercionist policy was not resolving the Irish question, or at least not quickly enough to avoid its becoming a major political liability. The lesson was clear — drop it.

Then there was the matter of prestige. The major stimulus behind criticism of the government's Irish policy was not concern for Ireland, but concern for England. It was in the tradition of Gladstone, holding that the treatment of Ireland disgraced England in the eyes of the world. The government was no less concerned with prestige, but its position was that it was defending the integrity and values of the Empire, the British way of life, and true humanity in Ireland against the assaults of assassins and destroyers. Its critics responded with the proposition that if the Empire and its values could be preserved only by counter-terror, then this was a negation of the principles being defended. At long last, in more than isolated instances, Englishmen were seeing English rule in Ireland as a contradiction of their own self-image, a revelation connected to the fact that the fashionable slogans of the day—'self-determination', 'rights of small nations', 'Prussianism', and the like—were being used by the Irish against the English. J. L. Hammond demanded an inquiry into reprisals—counter-terror—not only in the interests of Irishmen but because 'such an inquiry is demanded on the grounds of justice to the British people': he quoted the Irishman who had said to him, 'This is a tragedy . . ., but it is your tragedy, not ours'. What was happening in Ireland went against the English conviction that their rule stood for justice, liberty, peace, and the rule of law. It should therefore stop, even if this might seem to mean concessions to the violence of the Irish. At the same time, concessions must be at a minimum. The Treaty negotiations at the end of 1921 blended astute politicing with the threat of violence—'immediate and terrible war' should Ireland refuse to accept England's terms. Nor did the threat of English violence end there. The government remained prepared, into 1922, to declare war on Ireland if the symbol of the Crown was rejected by the Irish government and a republic proclaimed. 'If Ireland fell into a state of anarchy' Churchill stated in cabinet in May, 'we should have to re-establish a pale again around Dublin prior to reconquest'.

It has often been said in an Irish context, particularly by politicians and churchmen, that violence achieves nothing, save suffering and destruction; that it is at best futile, at worst a totally corruptive evil: the recent history of Northern Ireland is full of such statements. However one may wish such claims were true—for then, presumably, violence would be abandoned as ineffective as well as inhumane—they are demonstrably false, as Irish as well as other history consistently has shown. Violence can produce desired results. Between 1800 and 1921 England maintained its dominance of Ireland by violence and the threat of violence: this domination was terminated (or at least qualified) as a consequence of violence. And such reforms and positive changes as have occurred in Northern Ireland since 1968 are themselves the outcome of the pressure of violence. It may be that all of these things could have been achieved, and much more effectively, without violence. The point is that they were not — and in the use of violence, as in other forms of activity, nothing succeeds like success. Moreover, Irish history has been a continuing demonstration of the difficulty of getting changes and reforms by other means short of violence, or the threat thereof. It may be argued that what was in fact brought about by violence was about to occur through other means — for instance, that the 1916 rebellion pre-empted the success of a parliamentary movement about to achieve Home Rule. This must remain speculation. The actual lessons of Irish history point to violence as a salient constituent in the major changes in Anglo-Irish relations, lessons so prominent as hardly to be missed by those who wished to effect such changes.[4] The problem in coping with Irish violence came to be not only one of dealing with the long habit of violence, but of coping with the tendency of that violence to be ultimately successful in its objectives.

[4] Professor F. S. L. Lyons in relating historical analysis to contemporary concerns, has very properly condemned the assumption that 'Peaceful agitation and violent agitation are opposing poles with no resting place in between' as being a crude and naïve (not to say lethal) theory of society. He has stressed the many different and conflicting shades of opinion present in any crisis situation. See F.S.L. Lyons, 'From War to Civil War in Ireland. Three essays on the Treaty debate', in Brian Farrell (ed.) *The Irish Parliamentary Tradition* (Dublin, 1973). Although it is true, on the long view , that peaceful and violent agitation go together in the transformation of Irish society and of Anglo-Irish relations, the prominence of the violent element in effecting this has been such as to render difficult the task of those who, for moral and humane reasons, have insisted that action must remain constitutional. While it is true that violence has accumulated a mythological veneer which gives it a false heroic appeal and sham dignity, the real problem is not only that of destroying the myth, but of rendering violence futile. This would seem more likely to be achieved (if in fact it is achievable) by removing its excuses or rationale than by repression. While the immorality of individual violent acts may be clear, the question of the immorality of violence as part of the historical process might be another matter: 'Men are often more squeamish than God and more easily scandalized. They take exception to violence, although violence is one of the ways in which life bursts forth'. Jean Danielou, S.J., *Prayer as a Political Problem* (London, 1967) p. 106.

The obvious response, that of making sufficient (as against token) concessions to deprive violence of its rationale, is a relatively recent innovation in Anglo-Irish relations, dating from the pressure placed by the British government on the Northern Ireland government since 1968. However, such concessions must be made promptly in order to arrest the development of violence at a point short of that at which it becomes self-perpetuating and where it remains related to specific grievances. This did not occur. The Northern Ireland authorities were resistant to such conciliation, seeing coercion as the more appropriate policy, and taking a very different view from the British government on the problems of their society and of the nature of and motivation behind the threats to it; where the British saw legitimate civil liberties and social issues at stake, the Stormont authorities saw a threat to the security of the state, a state constituted according to the wishes of the vast majority.

The opportunity to remove the initial occasions of conflict and violence having passed, that violence began to escape in the later months of 1969 from the confines of the specific grievances that had occasioned it. It began to draw on the traditional sources of violence in Ulster — generations of fear and hatred, the desire for vengeance for past wrongs, real or imagined, and the mythologies of Protestant Unionism and Catholic nationalism. Violence came to be impelled less by present discontents than by the dynamic of the past. And at the same time as these factors peculiar to Northern Ireland became increasingly operative in sustaining and generating violence, the situation entered the so-called 'spiral of violence' phase. Established, institutionalized violence had provoked revolt. This had provoked repression, which itself became institutionalized — for instance in army occupation by 1970 and internment by 1971 — which became a new grievance provocative of revolt, and so on. In addition, the violence of that organization most prominent in the attack on the *status quo*, the IRA, prompted not only repressive violence from the arms of the established authorities, the police and army, but counter-terror from organizations of Protestant extremists.

In this complexity, the major problem was how to neutralize the main source of the violence. This was obviously the IRA. But the means which were used to pursue this, critics contended, were having precisely the opposite effect. Bishop Cathal Daly argued that 'Military counter-violence and internment have been the greatest promoters of physical force republicanism. They are still its strongest argument and the source of its greatest appeal'. There is no denying the counter-productive effect of at least two instances of counter-violence — the shooting of thirteen civilians in Derry by paratroops on 30 January 1972, and interrogation methods used on detainees — nor any doubt of the unpopularity of the British army with Catholic nationalists. But the matter was not simply one of discontinuing military counter-violence and internment. This could be transformatory only if, as Bishop Daly went on to insist, alienated Catholic areas were rid of the fear of attack from 'armed so-called "loyalists" '. Realistically it would seem that the only way this could be achieved would be a confrontation between the army and Protestant extremists of a kind no less prone to the operation of the 'spiral of violence' than what has occurred hitherto. To act effectively to attempt to neutralize either source of violence is to risk embedding it; not to act against both has the same effect. To act effectively against both at once is impossible, given the nature of the situation. In 1883 G. O. Trevelyan, then Irish Chief Secretary complained to his sister in terms which have some contemporary relevance to English attitudes:

'The effect of getting used to what is bad in Ireland is that you get more and more disgusted with the whole thing. The perversity of everybody who either writes or speaks is something inconceivable. If these people were left to themselves, we should have a mutual massacre; unless they are not quite as brave as they pretend.'

In these circumstances, attending to violence and attempting to end it becomes something other than using vigorous repression or remedying obvious causes.

Repression tends to maintain the violence or merely bury it. It becomes then a matter of reducing the level of violence to that where it is possible to sustain a relatively long-term programme of changing those attitudes and dispositions productive of violent conflict.

The difficulties in the way of achieving this are very considerable. It used to be believed, perhaps as late as the Northern Ireland election contests of 1973 and 1974, that violence itself would produce the necessary revulsion from extremism and create a massive moderate commonality of the centre which would itself be a major step towards the desired climate of change. This prediction failed to take account of several important factors in the situation. One is something of a general political law of development which says that the effect of violence and terror on 'ordinary', 'moderate' people is not to drive them towards moderation, but towards extremism. Taking up an extreme position accords not only with the intensity of the fears and hatreds which violence produces, but also with the increased desire for certainty and security: it thus inhibits movement from traditional outlooks and in fact confirms them. Nor did the hope that moderation would grow take account of how the potentially destructive effects of violence on the Northern Ireland economy were to be minimized. A major aim of the IRA campaign of property destruction was to create an economic crisis which would bring down the old political and social order. Massive compensation payments and injections of British capital ensured that this economic catastrophe did not occur. Although ordinary people were exposed to the risk of personal calamity, they were spared from economic calamity. And, of course, the more prosperous areas of the province escaped, in large part, the intensity of violence characteristic of central and west Belfast.

But perhaps more than anything else, the thesis that violence would produce a moderate reaction failed to take note of the grim fact that violence was far from being utterly discredited as an effective means of action in society. It can hardly be denied that in Irish history, violence traditionally expressed, in an extreme degree, the actual social relationships. As Bishop Daly put it in relation to Northern Ireland: 'The physical barricades simply reflect society as it has been shaped by its leaders and allowed to be shaped by its beneficiaries for 50 years.' In this sense, violence and counter-violence were natural, being merely a progression from the implicit conflicts and divisions to the explicit. To induce this process in reverse—that is, to return from violence to the modes of political resolution—is extremely difficult, for the existence of violence is testimony to the failure of politics to resolve the issues now in open conflict. The difficulty is greatly compounded if the movement beyond politics, into the realm of violence, has been accompanied by some measure of success. Then the lesson of experience has become that violence works, but politics do not. If the situation is such that those in conflict believe that they have still much to gain or lose, they will continue to resort to those means which have been proved to have served them best in crisis situations. In the case of both sides in Northern Ireland it has been actual violence, or willingness to resort to it, that has achieved most for them in the past. In 1910–14, Ulster Unionists secured the preservation of the Union, at least for themselves, by the threat of violence. In 1916–21 Catholic nationalists secured its partial severance by actual violence. More recently, the overthrow of the Stormont regime, undisturbed by any lesser pressures for fifty years, was a consequence of violence. That the disturbance of the Protestant *status quo* has not been far greater may reasonably be attributed to the known determination to defend it, if necessary by force. Calls for an end to violence, however strong their religious or humane appeal, are hard sayings indeed in a land where it seems that still so much remains to be gained or lost by violence.

These potential gains or losses—a united Ireland, or a Protestant province—may be judged as ideals or myths or perhaps absurd and dangerous irrelevancies. It would be foolish to deny their power to claim genuine allegiance and sacrifice, and to prompt violence deemed defensive and righteous: it would be equally blind to ignore those elements which are self-interested, criminal, or depraved. So far as what is genuine in this dynamic is concerned, part is derived from ideals or principles (misconceived though they may be); part is derived from the influences of the past. There is also, in the resort to or toleration of violence, the human instinct to seek a simple direct solution to problems of unbearable complexity. The attraction of violence is particularly great in situations where all other paths to a resolution which is secure and satisfactory are obscure and patently painful: violence offers the all or nothing gamble. Its opponents are hampered because they cannot offer any alternative which promises, however deceptively, such swift resolution, or promotes hallowed sectional slogans as complete solutions. Nor, given that violence has achieved so much, can they discredit it as a practical programme, other than by claiming that it brutalizes and degrades and that its human cost is greater than any possible political gains. Such arguments tend to fall on deaf ears, for those who are willing to use violence have embraced that morality which puts ends before means, or regard their principles as worth martyrdom, and are largely impervious to considerations of rationality which are peculiar to politics.

Whatever the future of that aspect of Anglo-Irish relations which remains—and the indications are that it may be one of protracted difficulty—the lessons of the past would seem to confirm a familiar historical theme: when the men of politics fail to accommodate the great problems and changes of their day, they will eventually be replaced as arbiters by the men of violence.

Select Bibliography

NOTE

The necessarily restricted selection of items for this bibliography has been designed to include those most important to further reading on aspects of the relationship between England and Ireland, those most relevant to the central themes and particular arguments of this book, and those most significant in relation to its sources. The present developing state of writing within this field is such as to demand the inclusion of a large number of recent journal articles: these are listed separately.

BOOKS

ARNOLD, MATTHEW. *English Literature and Irish Politics,* R. H. Super (ed.) The Complete Prose Works of Matthew Arnold, Vol. ix (Ann Arbor, 1973).

BAKER, SYBIL E. 'Orange and Green. Belfast 1832–1912', in H. J. Dyos and Michael Wolff (eds.) *The Victorian City. Images and Realities,* (London, 1973).

BARNETT, CORRELI. *The Collapse of British Power,* (London, 1972).

BARRITT, DENIS P. and CARTER, CHARLES F. *The Northern Ireland Problem. A Study in Group Relations,* 2nd ed. (London, 1972).

BECKETT, J. C. *The Making of Modern Ireland 1603–1923,* (London, 1966).

BEST, G. F. A. 'Popular Protestantism in Victorian Britain', in R. Robson (ed.) *Ideas and Institutions of Victorian Britain,* (London, 1967).

BLACK, R. D. C. *Economic Thought and The Irish Question 1817–1870,* (Cambridge, 1960).

BOWEN, ELIZABETH. *Bowen's Court,* (London, 1964).

BOWEN, ELIZABETH. *The Last September,* (London, 1929).

BOULTON, DAVID. *The U.V.F. 1966-73. An anatomy of loyalist rebellion,* (Dublin, 1973).

BOYCE, D. G. *Englishmen and Irish Troubles. British Public Opinion and the Making of Irish Policy 1918-22.* (London, 1972).

BOYCE, D. G. 'How to settle the Irish Question: Lloyd George and Ireland', in A. J. P. Taylor (ed.) *Lloyd George: Twelve Essays,* (London, 1971).

BOYD, ANDREW. *Holy War in Belfast,* (Tralee, 1969).

BROEKER, GALEN. *Rural Disorder and Police Reform in Ireland 1812-36,* (London, 1970).

BROWN, MALCOLM. *The Politics of Irish Literature. From Thomas Davis to W. B. Yeats,* (London, 1972).

BUCKLAND, PATRICK. *Irish Unionism,* Historical Association Pamphlet 81, (London, 1973).

BUCKLAND, PATRICK. *Irish Unionism: One. The Anglo-Irish and the New Ireland 1885-1922,* (Dublin, 1972).

BUCKLAND, PATRICK, *Irish Unionism: Two. Ulster Unionism and the Origins of Northern Ireland 1886-1922,* (Dublin, 1973).

BULFIN, WILLIAM. *Rambles in Eirinn,* 2nd ed., (Dublin, 1920).

BURKE, THOMAS H. *Lectures on Faith and Fatherland,* (London, n.d.).

CAHILL, REV. E. *The Framework of a Christian State: an introduction to social science,* (Dublin, 1932).

CALLAGHAN, JAMES. *A House Divided. The Dilemma of Northern Ireland,* (London, 1973).

CARLYLE, THOMAS. *English and other Critical Essays,* Everyman's ed. (London, 1964).

CARLYLE, THOMAS. *Reminiscences of My Irish Journey in 1849,* (London, 1882).

CONNELL, K. H. *Irish Peasant Society. Four Historical Essays,* (Oxford, 1968).

CORISH, P. 'Political Problems 1860-1878', in P. Corish (ed.) *A History of Irish Catholicism,* Vol. 5, fascicule 3, (Dublin, 1967).

COWLING, MAURICE, *The Impact of Labour 1920-1924,* (Cambridge, 1971).

CROSLAND, T. W. H. *The Wild Irishman,* (London, 1905).

CULLEN, L. M. *An Economic History of Ireland since 1660,* (London, 1972).

CULLEN, L. M. (ed.). *The Formation of the Irish Economy,* (Cork, 1969).

CURTIS, L. P. *Anglo-Saxons and Celts*, (New York, 1968).

CURTIS, L. PERRY, JR. *Apes and Angels. The Irishman in Victorian Caricature*, (Newton Abbot, 1971).

CURTIS, L. P. *Coercion and Conciliation in Ireland 1880-1892. A Study in Conservative Unionism*, (Princeton, 1963).

CUSACK, M. F. *The Present Case of Ireland Plainly Stated; A Plea for my People and my Race*, (New York, 1883).

DALY, CATHAL B. *Violence in Ireland*, (Dublin, 1973). —

DANGERFIELD, GEORGE. *The Strange Death of Liberal England*, (London, 1935).

DANIELOU, JEAN. *Prayer as a Political Problem*, (London, 1967).

DENVIR, JOHN. *The Irish in Britain from the Earliest Time to the Fall and Death of Parnell*, (London, 1892).

DEVLIN, BERNADETTE. *The Price of my Soul*, (London, 1969).

DILLON, MARTIN and LEHANE, DENIS. *Political Murder in Northern Ireland*, (Penguin, 1973).

EDWARDS, R. DUDLEY. *A New History of Ireland*, (Dublin, 1972).

EDWARDS, R. DUDLEY and WILLIAMS, T. DESMOND (eds.). *The Great Famine. Studies in Irish History 1845-52*, (Dublin, 1956).

EVANS, E. ESTYN. *The Personality of Ireland. Habitat, Heritage and History*, (Cambridge, 1973).

FITZGERALD, GARRETT. *Towards a New Ireland*, (London, 1972).

FOX, J. A. *A Key to the Irish Question. Mainly compiled from the Speeches and Writings of Eminent British Statesmen and Publicists, Past and Present*, (London, 1890).

GILLEY, SHERIDAN. 'Catholic Faith of the Irish Slums, London, 1840-70', in H. J. Dyos and Michael Wolff (eds.). *The Victorian City. Images and Realities*, (London, 1973).

GILLEY, SHERIDAN. 'Papists, Protestants and the Irish in London 1835-70', in G. J. Cuming and Derek Baker (eds.). *Popular Belief and Practice*, (Cambridge, 1972).

GOLLIN, A. M. *Proconsul in Politics. A Study of Lord Milner in Opposition and in Power*, (London, 1963).

GOOD, JAMES WINDER. *Ulster and Ireland*, (Dublin, 1919).

GWYNN, DENIS. 'Great Britain: England and Wales', in P. Corish (ed.), *A History of Irish Catholicism* Vol. vi, fascicule 1 (Dublin, 1968).

GWYNN, DENIS. 'The Irish Immigration', in G. A. Beck (ed.) *The English Catholics 1850-1950*, (London, 1950).

HAMILTON, ERNEST. *The Soul of Ulster,* (London, 1917).

HANCOCK, W. K. *Survey of British Commonwealth Affairs*, Vol. 1 'Problems of Nationality', (London, 1937).

HANDLEY, JAMES E. 'Great Britain: Scotland', in P. Corish (ed.) *A A History of Irish Catholicism*, Vol. vi fascicule 1, (Dublin, 1968).

HANDLEY, JAMES E. *The Irish in Modern Scotland*, (Cork, 1947).

HARBINSON, JOHN. *The Ulster Unionist Party 1882-1973*, (Belfast, 1973).

HARKNESS, D. W. *The Restless Dominion. The Irish Free State and the British Commonwealth of Nations*, 1921-31, (London, 1969).

HARRIS, ROSEMARY. *Prejudice and tolerance in Ulster. A study of neighbours and 'strangers' in a border community*, (Manchester, 1972).

HAY, IAN. *The Oppressed English*, (London, 1918).

HICKEY, JOHN. *Urban Catholics. Urban Catholicism in England and Wales from 1829 to the present day*, (London, 1967).

INGLIS, BRIAN. *Roger Casement*, (London, 1973).

JACKSON, J. A. *The Irish in Britain*, (London, 1963).

JAMES, FRANCIS GODWIN. *Ireland and the Empire 1688-1770*, (Cambridge, Massachusetts, 1973).

JONES, THOMAS. *Whitehall Diary*, Vol. III, Ireland 1918-1925, (London, 1971).

KEE, ROBERT. *The Green Flag. A History of Irish Nationalism*, (London, 1972).

LEE, JOSEPH. *The Modernisation of Irish Society, 1848-1918*, (Dublin, 1973).

LOFTUS, RICHARD J. *Nationalism in Modern Anglo-Irish Poetry*, (Madison and Milwaukee, 1964).

LONGFORD, LORD, (Frank Packenham). *Peace by Ordeal*, Paperback ed. (London, 1972).

LYONS, F. S. L. 'From War to Civil War in Ireland. Three essays on the Treaty debate', in Brian Farrell (ed.) *The Irish Parliamentary Tradition*, (Dublin, 1973).

LYONS, F. S. L. *Ireland Since the Famine*, rev. ed. (London, 1973).

MCCAFFREY, LAWRENCE J. *The Irish Question 1800-1922*, (Kentucky, 1968).

MCCANN, EAMONN. *The British Press and Northern Ireland*, (London, n.d. [1971]).

MCCANN, EAMONN. *War and an Irish Town*, (Penguin, 1974).

MCCARTNEY, DONAL. 'James Anthony Froude and Ireland: a Historiographical Controversy in the Nineteenth Century', in T. D. Williams (ed.) *Historical Studies. Papers read before the Irish Conference of Historians VIII Dublin 27-30 May 1969*, (Dublin, 1971).

MACDONAGH, OLIVER, *Ireland,* (New Jersey, 1968).

MACDONAGH, OLIVER. *The Nineteenth Century Novel and Irish Social History*, O'Donnell Lecture delivered at University College, Cork on April 21st 1970, (Dublin, 1970).

MCDOWELL, R. B. *British Conservatism 1832-1914*, (London, 1959).

MCDOWELL, R. B. *Public Opinion and Government Policy in Ireland 1801-1846*, (London, 1952).

MCDOWELL, R. B. *The Irish Administration 1801-1914*, (London, 1964).

MCGUFFIN, JOHN. *Internment*, (Tralee, 1973).

MACVEIGH, JEREMIAH. *Home Rule in A Nutshell. A Pocket Book for Speakers and Electors*, (Dublin and London, 1911).

MAGUIRE, J. F. *The Irish in America,* (London, 1868).

MAGUIRE, W. A. *The Downshire Estates in Ireland 1801-1845. The management of Irish landed estates in the early nineteenth century*, (Oxford, 1972).

MANSERGH, NICHOLAS. 'Ireland and the British Commonwealth of Nations: the Dominion Settlement', in Desmond Williams (ed.) *The Irish Struggle 1916-1926,* (London, 1966).

MANSERGH, NICHOLAS. 'Ireland: External Relations 1926-1939', in Francis MacManus (ed.), *The Years of the Great Test,* (Cork, 1967).

MANSERGH, NICHOLAS. 'Irish Foreign Policy, 1945-51', in Kevin B. Nowlan and T. Desmond Williams, *Ireland in the War Years and After 1939-51*, (Dublin, 1969).

MANSERGH, NICHOLAS. *The Government of Northern Ireland*, (London, 1936).

MANSERGH, NICHOLAS. *The Irish Question 1840-1921*, (London, 1965).

MARRINAN, PATRICK. *Paisley. Man of Wrath*, (Tralee, 1973).

MARTIN, F. X. and BYRNE, F. J. (eds.). *The Scholar Revolutionary: Eoin MacNeill, 1867-1945, and the Making of the New Ireland*, (Shannon, 1973).

MARTIN, HUGH. *Ireland in Insurrection. An Englishman's Record*, (London, 1921).

MARX, KARL and ENGELS, FREDERICK. *On Ireland*, (London, 1971).

MATTHEW, H. C. G. *The Liberal Imperialists*, (Oxford, 1973).

MIDDLETON, THE EARL OF, *Ireland—Dupe or Heroine*, (London, 1932).

MILLER, DAVID W. *Church, State and Nation in Ireland 1898-1921*, (Dublin, 1973).

MITCHEL, JOHN. *The Last Conquest of Ireland (Perhaps)*, (Glasgow, n.d.).

MOLONY, J. CHARTRES. *Ireland's Tragic Comedians*, (London, 1934).

MOORE, BARRINGTON, JR. *Social Origins of Dictatorship and Democracy. Lord and Peasant in the Making of the Modern World*, (Peregrine, 1969).

MOWAT, C. L. 'The Irish Question in British Politics (1916-1922)', in Desmond Williams (ed.) *The Irish Struggle 1916-1926*, (London, 1966).

MURRAY, ALICE E. *A History of the Commercial and Financial Relations between England and Ireland from the period of the Restoration*, New ed., (London, 1907).

NORMAN, EDWARD. *A History of Modern Ireland*, (London, 1971).

NORMAN, E. R. *Anti-Catholicism in Victorian England*, (London, 1968).

NORMAN, E. R. *The Catholic Church and Ireland in the Age of Rebellion 1859-1873*, (London, 1965).

O'BRIEN, C. C. *States of Ireland* (London, 1972).

Ó BROIN, LEON. *Dublin Castle and the 1916 Rising*, (Dublin, 1966).

Ó BROIN, LEON. *Fenian Fever. An Anglo-American Dilemma*, (London, 1971).

Ó BROIN, LEON. *The Chief Secretary. Augustine Birrell in Ireland*, (London, 1969).

O'CONNOR, KEVIN, *The Irish in Britain*, (London, 1972).

O'CONNOR, T. P. 'The Irish in Great Britain', in F. Lavery (comp.) *Great Irishmen in War and Politics*, (London, 1920).

O'DRISCOLL, ROBERT, (ed.). *Theatre and nationalism in twentieth-century Ireland*, (London, 1971).

O'FARRELL, PATRICK. *Ireland's English Question. Anglo-Irish Relations 1534-1970*, (London, 1971).

O'HEGARTY, P. S. *The Victory of Sinn Fein*, (Dublin, 1924).

PACKENHAM, FRANK. 'The Treaty Negotiations', in Desmond Williams (ed.), *The Irish Struggle 1916-1926*, (London, 1966).

PEARSE, PADRAIC H. *Political Writings and Speeches*, (Dublin, 1962 printing).

POWELL, J. ENOCH, *Still to Decide*, (London, 1972).

QUINN, D. B. *The Elizabethans and the Irish*, (New York, 1966).

RIDDELL, PATRICK. *Fire over Ulster*, (London, 1970).

ROSE, PAUL. *The Manchester Martyrs. The Story of a Fenian Tragedy*, (London, 1970).

ROSE, RICHARD. *Governing without Consensus. An Irish Perspective*, (London, 1971).

SEMMEL, BERNARD (ed.). *Occasional Papers of T. R. Malthus*, (New York, 1963).

SHEEHAN, P. A. *Luke Delmege*, (London, 1935 ed.).

SOLOW, BARBARA LEWIS. *The Land Question and the Irish Economy, 1870-1903*, (Cambridge, Massachusetts, 1971).

SMYTH, TONY. *Northern Ireland. The Mailed Fist. A Record of Army & Police Brutality from Aug. 9-Nov. 9 1971*, (Antrim, 1971).

STEELE, E. D. *Irish Land and British Politics*, (Cambridge, 1974).

STRAUSS, E. *Irish Nationalism and British Democracy*, (London, 1951).

SUNDAY TIMES INSIGHT TEAM. *Ulster*, (Penguin, 1972).

The Ulster Debate: Report of a Study Group of the Institute for the Study of Conflict, (London, 1972).

THOMPSON, E. P. *The Making of the English Working Class*, (London, 1963).

THOMPSON, W. I. *The Imagination of an Insurrection: Dublin, Easter 1916*, (New York, 1967).

TUCHMAN, BARBARA W. *The Proud Tower. A Portrait of the World before the War: 1890-1914*, (London, 1966).

WARD, WILFRED. *The Life of John Henry Cardinal Newman*, (London, 1912).

WEST, REBECCA. *The Meaning of Treason*, (Penguin, 1965).

WHITE, TERENCE DE VERE. *The Anglo-Irish*, (London, 1972).

WHYTE, J. H. *Church and State in Modern Ireland 1923-70*, (Dublin, 1971).

WHYTE, J. H. 'Political Problems, 1850-1860', in P. Corish (ed.) *A History of Irish Catholicism*, Vol. 5, fascicule 2, (Dublin, 1967).

YEATS, W. B. *Tribute to Thomas Davis*, (Cork, 1947).

ARTICLES

BELL, J. BOWYER. 'The Chroniclers of Violence: The Troubles in Northern Ireland Interpreted', *Eire-Ireland* viii, i, Spring 1972.

BLACK, R. D. COLLINSON. 'Economic Policy in Ireland and India in the Time of J. S. Mill', *Economic History Review*, 2nd ser., xxi, 2, (Aug. 1968).

BOYLE, JOHN W. 'Irish Labor and the Rising', *Eire-Ireland*, ii, 3, (Autumn 1967).

BROMAGE, MARY C. 'Image of Nationhood', *Eire-Ireland*, iii, 3, (Autumn 1968).

BUCKLAND, P. J. 'The southern Irish unionists, the Irish question, and British politics, 1906-14', *Irish Historical Studies*, xv, 59, (March 1867).

BUTLIN, NOEL G. 'A New Plea for the Separation of Ireland', *Journal of Economic History*, 28, 1, (March 1968).

CAHILL, GILBERT A. 'Irish Catholicism and English Toryism', *Review of Politics*, 19, (Jan. 1957).

CAHILL, GILBERT. 'Some Nineteenth-century Roots of the Ulster Problem, 1829-1848', *Irish University Review*, 1, (1970).

CAHILL, GILBERT A. 'The Protestant Association and the Anti-Maynooth Agitation of 1845', *Catholic Historical Review*, xliii, 3, (October 1957).

CANNY, NICHOLAS P. 'The Ideology of English Colonisation: From England to America', *William and Mary Quarterly*, 3rd series, xxx, 4, (October 1973).

COOKE, A. B. and VINCENT, J. R. 'Select documents; xxvii Ireland and party politics, 1885-7: an unpublished Conservative memoir (I)', *Irish Historical Studies*, xvi, 62, (September 1968).

COOKE, A. B. and VINCENT, J. R. 'Select documents: xxvii Ireland and party politics, 1885-7: an unpublished Conservative memoir (II)', *Irish Historical Studies*, xvi, 63, (March 1969).

CULLEN, L. M. 'The Hidden Ireland: Re-Assessment of a Concept', *Studia Hibernia*, 9, (1969).

FAIR, JOHN D. 'The Anglo-Irish Treaty of 1921: Unionist Aspects of the Peace', *Journal of British Studies*, xii, 1, (November 1972).

FANNING, RONAN. 'The unionist party and Ireland 1906-10', *Irish Historical Studies*, xv, 58, (September 1966).

GILLEY, SHERIDAN. 'Protestant London, No Popery and the Irish Poor 1830-60', *Recusant History*, 10, (1970).

GILLEY, SHERIDAN. 'Protestant London, No Popery and the Irish Poor: II (1850-1860)', *Recusant History*, 11, (1971).

GILLEY, SHERIDAN. 'The Roman Catholic Mission to the Irish in London, 1840-1860', *Recusant History*, 10, (1969).

GRIFFITHS, A. R. G. 'The Irish Board of Works in the Famine Years', *Historical Journal* xiii, 4, (1970).

HAMER, D. A. 'The Irish Question and Liberal Politics, 1886-1894', *Historical Journal* xii, 3, (1969).

HERNON, JOSEPH M. JR. 'The Historian as Politician: G. O. Trevelyan as Irish Chief Secretaty', *Eire-Ireland*, viii, 3, (Autumn 1973).

HOPPEN, K. THEODORE. 'Tories, Catholics and the General Election of 1859', *Historical Journal*, xiii, 1, (1970).

HOWARD, C. H. D. 'Select documents: xxvi 'The man on a tricycle': W. H. Duignan and Ireland, 1881-5', *Irish Historical Studies*, xiv, 55, (March 1965).

HURST, MICHAEL. 'Ireland and the Ballot Act of 1872', *Historical Journal* viii, 3, (1965).

JONES, W. R. 'England Against the Celtic Fringe: a study in Cultural Stereotypes', *Journal of World History*, xiii, 1, (1971).

JONES, W. R. '*Giraldus Redivivus* — English Historians, Irish Apologists, and the Works of Gerald of Wales', *Eire-Ireland*, ix, 3, (Autumn 1973).

JUPP, P. J. 'Irish Parliamentary Elections and the Influence of the Catholic Vote, 1801-20', *Historical Journal*, x, 2, (1967).

KEEP, G. R. C. 'Official Opinion on Irish Emigration in the later 19th Century', *Irish Ecclesiastical Record*, 5th Series, lxxxi, (June 1954).

KRIEGEL, A. D. 'The Irish policy of Lord Grey's government', *English Historical Review*, lxxxvi, (January 1971).

LARKIN, E. 'Church and State in Ireland in the Nineteenth Century', *Church History*, xxxi, (September 1962).

LARKIN, EMMET. 'The Devotional Revolution in Ireland, 1850-75', *American Historical Review*, 77, 3, (June 1972).

LEA, JOHN. 'W. S. Caine and Irish Home Rule — A Study of the Radical Opposition of 1886', *History Studies*, I, 2, (1968).

LEBOW, NED. 'British Historians and Irish History', *Eire-Ireland*, viii, 4, (Winter 1973).

MCCAFFREY, JOHN. 'The Irish Vote in Glasgow in the Later Nineteenth Century. A Preliminary Survey', *The Innes Review*, 21, (1970).

MCCARTNEY, DONAL. 'Lecky's *Leaders of public opinion in Ireland*', *Irish Historical Studies*, xiv, 54, (September 1964).

MCCORD, NORMAN. 'The Fenians and Public Opinion in Great Britain', *University Review*, (Dublin) 4, (1967).

MCEWEN, JOHN N. 'The Liberal Party and the Irish Question during the First World War', *Journal of British Studies*, xii, 1, (November 1972).

RICHTER, MICHAEL. 'The First Century of Anglo-Irish Relations', *History*, 59, 196, (June 1974).

ROSE, RICHARD. 'Ulster Politics: A Select Bibliography of Political Discord', *Political Studies*, xx, (June 1972).

SAVAGE, DONALD C. 'The Irish Unionists: 1867-1886', *Eire-Ireland*, ii, 3, (Autumn 1967).

SAVAGE, D. C. 'The Origins of the Ulster Unionist Party 1885-6', *Irish Historical Studies*, xii, (1960-61).

SAVAGE, DAVID W. 'The Attempted Home Rule Settlement of 1916', *Eire-Ireland*, ii, 3, (Autumn 1967).

SAVAGE, DAVID W. 'The Parnell of Wales has become the Chamberlain of England: Lloyd George and the Irish Question', *Journal of British Studies*, xii, 1, (November 1972).

SHAW, FRANCIS. 'The Canon of Irish History—A Challenge', *Studies*, Lxi, 242, (Summer 1972).

STEELE, E. D. 'Gladstone and Ireland', *Irish Historical Studies*, xvii, 65, (March 1970).

STEELE, E. D. 'Ireland and the Empire in the 1860s. Imperial Precedents for Gladstone's First Irish Land Act', *Historical Journal*, xi, 1 (1968).

STEELE, E. D. 'J. S. Mill and the Irish Question: The Principles of Political Economy, 1848-1865', *Historical Journal*, xiii, 2, (1970).

STEELE, E. D. 'J. S. Mill and the Irish Question: Reform, and the Integrity of the Empire, 1865-1870', *Historical Journal*, xiii, 3, (1970).

SWEENEY, JOSEPH. 'Why "Sinn Fein"?', *Eire-Ireland*, vi, 2, (Summer 1971).

THOMPSON, E. P. 'The Moral Economy of the English Crowd in the Eighteenth Century', *Past and Present*, 50 (February 1971).

WALKER, R. B. 'Religious Changes in Liverpool in the Nineteenth Century', *Journal of Ecclesiastical History*, xix, 2, (October 1968).

WERLY, JOHN. 'The Irish in Manchester, 1832-49', *Irish Historical Studies*, xvii, 71, (March 1973).

WOODS, C. J. 'Anti-Irish Intrigue at the Vatican', *Eire-Ireland*, iv, 2, (Summer 1969).

WOODS, C. J. 'Ireland and Anglo-papal relations 1880-85', *Irish Historical Studies*, xviii, 69, (March 1972).

Index